Launch Your Bookkeeping Business

Barry Robertson

Published by Barry Robertson, 2025.

LAUNCH YOUR BOOKKEEPING BUSINESS

First edition. November 4, 2025.

ISBN: 979-8232536893

Written by Barry Robertson.

Table of Contents

Introduction

Why the First 10 Clients Are the Most Difficult to Get (and the Most Important)

Securing your first ten clients as a newly certified bookkeeper can feel like climbing a steep hill in the rain. It can be daunting, slow-going and full of uncertainty. You won't just be building a list of clients. You'll be building trust, credibility and confidence - both in yourself and in the eyes of others.

At this early stage, you'll be likely to face a perfect storm of challenges:

- **No portfolio to showcase**

  With you having no track record, prospects can't see proof of your skills. You'll be asking them to take a leap of faith.

- **No referrals to show**

  In the bookkeeping world, referrals are like gold. It's only once you have a few happy clients under your belt that the referrals start flowing in.

- **Imposter syndrome**

  Even with your certification in hand, you might still wonder if you're "ready" or not. That self-doubt can quietly sabotage your outreach and confidence in pricing.

- **Unclear messaging**

  New bookkeepers sometimes struggle to articulate what makes them different or valuable. Without a clear offer, it's easy to blend into the background.

In spite of such hurdles, *your first ten clients are the most important you'll ever land.* Why? Because they will form the foundation of whatever comes after. They give you:

- **Testimonials and case studies** to build your credibility

- **Referrals and repeat business** to reduce your future marketing efforts

- **Clarity and confidence** in your niche, pricing and process

- **Momentum** - the most potent force in any new business

Think of these first ten as your proving ground. Once you've served them well, the next ten will come faster. And the ten after that? Even faster still. It all starts with determination, strategy and a willingness to get stuck in before you feel fully ready.

Setting Timelines and the Effort Required

Try to be realistic. Getting your first ten clients won't happen overnight. You will have to apply consistent effort, critical thinking and a willingness to step outside your comfort zone.

For most new bookkeepers, a timeline for securing ten paying clients could typically be between three and six months. Some may move more rapidly, especially if they have prior business experience. Others may take longer if they have other commitments or are starting from scratch.

Drive is more important than speed. Every conversation, outreach and small victory brings you closer to your objective. The key is to stay active and goal-oriented.

Here's what you'll need to prepare yourself for:

- **2–5 hours per week** of focused client-building activity

  This includes networking, marketing, follow-ups and refining your messaging.

- **A willingness to experiment**

  Not every tactic will work for you — and that's okay. This book will help you test and adapt quickly.

- **Resilience and consistency**

  You'll face rejection, silence and slow days. Your job is to keep showing up anyway.

- **A mindset of service**

  When you focus on helping rather than selling, people respond. Your first ten clients are out there — they just need to know you exist.

This book is designed to help you maximise your effort, minimise wasted time and build traction week by week. If you commit to the process, those ten clients will come — and they'll be the start of something much bigger.

Chapter 1: Positioning Yourself as a Professional

Before you fire off that email or hit "post" on social media, take a second and ask yourself—why would anyone hand their books over to you?

It's not about faking it or playing a role. It's about showing people what you're really good at, and doing it with some confidence. You don't want to be just another bookkeeper in the crowd. You want people to see you as someone they can count on—a real financial partner.

1.1 Define Your Professional Identity

Get specific about who you are and what you bring to the table. Who do you work with? Maybe you help sole traders, tradespeople, or small limited companies. What's your style? Are you all about the details, or do you focus more on advice and strategy? What matters to you—accuracy, transparency, keeping things simple or helping people feel empowered?

Try putting that into a quick statement that sums up what you do. Something that feels honest and straightforward. Here's a suggestion:

> *"I help small business owners stay financially organised and confident by providing a clear, reliable bookkeeping service that's tailored to their needs."*

Make this statement the backbone of your messaging — from your website to your business proposals.

1.2 Present Yourself Professionally

You don't need a fancy brand right out of the gate but you do need to look legit. Start with a **professional email**—skip the free personal stuff and go for something like yourname@yourbusiness.com. Set up a simple website or landing page. Nothing complicated, just a clean, one-page site with your services, your contact info, and a decent photo of yourself.

Don't forget **LinkedIn.** Polish your profile with a clear headline, a solid summary and a photo that looks both friendly and professional. Keep your branding consistent—same colors, fonts and tone everywhere. People notice that kind of thing. First impressions stick, so make sure yours says, "*I mean business*".

1.3 Build Trust Signals

When you're just starting out, people want to know you're the real deal. So, show them. Talk about your **qualifications** and any professional groups you're part of. Tell your story—why did you decide to become a bookkeeper in the first place? People connect with honesty.

Share useful tips, break down common mistakes or offer insights about the job. That kind of content proves you know what you're doing. And don't wait to ask for **testimonials**. Even a few nice words from a volunteer client or a supportive peer can make a big difference. Trust doesn't show up overnight but every little thing you do helps build it.

1.4 Adopt a Professional Mindset

In the end, professionalism isn't just about appearances—it's a mindset. It's about respecting your time and **setting boundaries**. Charge what your work is worth, even when you're just starting out. **Be clear and dependable** when you communicate. Own your work, and always keep learning. When you take yourself seriously, people notice and do the same.

Now, about tools: When you're new to bookkeeping, you'll want to streamline your tech setup. You'll need cloud bookkeeping software, secure ways to share files and some basic tools to manage clients and schedules. That's really all you need to get rolling.

Here's a practical breakdown of the **core tools and software** every newly certified bookkeeper should consider:

Bookkeeping and Accounting Software

These are your everyday tools—they let you handle client accounts, keep track of transactions and pull up reports without a headache.

Xero is a favourite in a lot of places. It's easy to use, great for small businesses and gives you handy features like bank feeds, invoicing and VAT support.

QuickBooks Online is everywhere. People love its flexibility, how easily it connects with other apps and the fact that you can use it on your phone.

FreeAgent works really well for freelancers and tiny businesses, especially if you deal with UK taxes.

Sage Accounting? Tons of firms trust it. It's packed with features and it's strong enough to keep up as your business grows.

Here's a tip: pick one platform, get really good at it and treat it as your specialty. You can always add more tools to your belt later.

2. Document Management & File Sharing

You need a safe way to share sensitive financial documents with your clients.

Google Workspace or **Microsoft 365** both work well for email, cloud storage (think Google Drive or OneDrive) and for working together on documents.

If you want secure file sharing with options to set folder permissions and track activity, **Dropbox or Box** are good choices. For editing, signing and organizing PDFs, go with **Adobe Acrobat** or **PDFescape**.

3. Scheduling & Calendar Tools

If you want to stay on top of meetings, deadlines and all those repeating tasks, here's what actually helps:

Calendly lets your clients grab a slot on your calendar. No more endless back-and-forth.

Google Calendar or **Outlook** keep everything in sync with your email and send you reminders so nothing slips through the cracks.

Trello and **Asana** make it easy to track where each client is in the onboarding process and can keep your team's workflow organized.

4. Communication Tools

Now, about communication—being clear and professional really does make a difference.

For meetings or client calls, **Zoom** and **Microsoft Teams** are your go-tos.

When you just need a quick update or want a casual chat, **Slack** or **WhatsApp Business** work well (if that's what your clients like).

And don't forget your email signature—tools like **Wisestamp** give your messages that extra bit of polish.

5. CRM & Client Management

Even if you only have a handful of clients, staying organized really matters.

HubSpot CRM's free version lets you track leads, conversations and follow-ups without much hassle.

Notion or **Airtable** work great as flexible databases—you can use them to keep track of client details, deadlines and notes, all in one place.

6. Security & Compliance

When you're dealing with financial data, you have to keep it safe.

Try a password manager like **LastPass** or **Bitwarden** to lock down your logins.

Turn on two-factor authentication for every account you use.

And don't forget about **GDPR compliance tools** if you're storing client data online—privacy rules aren't optional.

Key Takeaway:

Don't just rush into pitching—start by positioning yourself. That first impression? It shapes every client relationship you'll have so make it matter.

Setting Up Your Business Legally (U.S. Edition)

Now, before you take on your first client, get your business set up the right way. In the U.S., that means picking the **business structure** that fits, getting the right **insurance** and using solid **contracts**. These steps don't just keep you safe—they show clients you're serious and help everyone trust the process.

1. Choose Your Business Structure

If you're a bookkeeper in the US, you have a few main ways to set up your business:

Sole Proprietorship

This one's as simple as it gets. You just work under your own name or pick a DBA ("doing business as"). Hardly any paperwork. The catch? You're on the hook personally if anything goes wrong—debts, lawsuits, you name it.

Limited Liability Company (LLC)

Lots of freelancers and small business owners go this route. An LLC protects your personal stuff—like your car or savings—if your business runs into trouble. Setting one up isn't a headache and you get some wiggle room with taxes.

S Corporation (S-Corp)

If you're making decent money and want to cut down on self-employment tax, this setup makes sense. There's definitely more paperwork and rules to follow but, as your income grows, it can save you a good chunk of cash.

Tip: Most new bookkeepers go with an LLC because it offers good protection without making things complicated. You can set one up through your state's Secretary of State website or just use a service like LegalZoom or Incfile if you want it done fast.

2. Secure the Right Insurance

Don't skip **insurance**, even if you work from home. It's not just about staying safe from unexpected claims—it also tells your clients you mean business.

Professional Liability Insurance (Errors & Omissions) covers you if a client says he lost money because of something you missed or messed up. You need this.

General Liability Insurance takes care of things like accidental injuries or damage to property, especially if you meet clients face-to-face or go to networking events.

Cyber Liability Insurance kicks in if there's a data breach, hacking or loss of sensitive financial info.

A Business Owner's Policy (BOP) wraps general liability and property coverage into one. That's handy if you have a home office or use your own equipment.

Tip: It's smart to talk to an insurance broker who actually knows the financial services world. He can help you figure out exactly what coverage fits your situation.

3. Use Contracts and Engagement Letters

Please don't start working without a written agreement. A contract isn't just paperwork—it protects you and your client and makes sure everyone knows what to expect right from the start.

Your contract (or engagement letter, if you call it that) needs to spell out a few key things: what you'll do and what you won't, how and when you'll get paid, how you both handle confidentiality and what happens if things need to end early. Don't forget a plan for resolving disagreements, plus what you'll need from your client to do your job correctly.

If you're not sure where to start, check out templates from groups like the American Institute of Professional Bookkeepers or the National Association of Certified Public Bookkeepers. Honestly, it's smart to get a lawyer to look over your agreement—better safe than sorry.

One last tip: add a clause that lets you use anonymised testimonials or case studies. It's a simple way to help your marketing down the road.

4. Register for Taxes and Compliance

What you need to do depends on your state and how your business is set up. You'll probably need to get an Employer Identification Number (EIN) from the IRS—even if you're running things solo. Most states also want you to **register your business** with their Department of Revenue. If you sell goods, you might have to collect and send in sales tax but this usually isn't a bookkeeping thing—still, double-check your state's rules just to be sure.

If you have an **LLC or a corporation**, expect to file annual reports or renew your registration every year. On top of that, you'll need to stay on top of IRS and state tax filings, including those quarterly estimated taxes.

If you're dealing with client funds or running payroll, you might need to follow Money Services Business (MSB) regulations or get a surety bond, depending on your state. It sounds like a lot but keeping up with these steps keeps your business legit.

Key Takeaway:

Setting up your business the right way isn't just about ticking boxes. It's about building trust from the ground up. With your structure, insurance and contracts sorted, you can pitch your services confidently and actually enjoy delivering on your promises.

Chapter 2: Pricing Without Experience

The Beginner Pricing Dilemma

One of the toughest questions new bookkeepers run into is, "*How much should I charge?*" When you don't have a portfolio, reviews or much experience, it's easy to feel as if you have no bargaining power. That feeling can make you freeze up, second-guess yourself or just lowball your prices because you want the work so badly.

But here's the thing: pricing isn't only about how many years you've been doing this. It's about the value you bring, how you present yourself and, honestly, how much confidence you can muster.

Why does pricing feel like such a minefield when you're starting out? For one, there's that nagging imposter syndrome — "*Who am I to charge real money for this?*" Then there's the fear: "*If I ask for too much, they'll just find someone else.*" On top of that, you probably have no idea what others are charging so you're guessing. Sometimes you just want to get going so you tell yourself, "*I'll start cheap and raise my rates later.*"

All of these thoughts are normal but they can trap you in a cycle of undercharging and undervaluing your own work. If you're not careful, you end up building a business that eats up your time and energy without giving much back.

The Risk of Underpricing

Charging too little sounds like an easy way to land clients but, honestly, it usually backfires. You end up working with people who care more about price than quality. They're quick to question your fees and slow to see your value. If you try to raise your rates later, get ready for pushback. And delivering great service for bargain prices? That's a fast track to burnout. Whether you mean to or not, low prices send a message: "I'm not sure my work is worth more."

Here's the thing—your price shapes how people see you. If you don't respect your own time and skills, why would anyone else?

What Are You Really Charging For?

Even if you're new, you're offering a lot more than number-crunching. You're giving clients peace of mind so they can actually sleep at night knowing that their finances are in good hands. You're saving them hours they can pour back into their business. You help them avoid mistakes that could cost real money. You show up, do what you say and keep the lines of communication open. That kind of reliability is rare—and it's worth real money. Don't sell yourself short.

Reframing the Dilemma

Stop asking yourself, "*What am I worth?*" and start thinking, "*What's this service actually worth to my client? And how can I show up with confidence and deliver that?*"

You don't have to be the cheapest option out there. What matters is being clear, consistent and building trust.

Here's the bottom line: Pricing is not easy when you're new but it's doable. Focus on the value you bring, not how long you've been doing it. Those first clients? They aren't paying for your résumé — they want results. Give them that.

Setting Your First Rates

Figuring out how much to charge when you're just starting out feels a bit like guessing with your eyes closed. You want your prices to be fair, you want to look professional and, let's be real, you don't want to scare off clients by asking for too much—or too little. The truth? You don't need years of experience to price your services like you know what you're doing. What really matters is having a solid plan and knowing the value you bring.

Start with a range, not just one magic number.

Don't stress about finding the one "right" rate. Pick a range that makes sense for what you do. For freelance bookkeepers in the U.S., you'll usually see numbers like these to kick things off:

$25–$40 an hour for basic bookkeeping tasks.

$300–$600 a month if you're handling regular work for a small business.

$150–$300 per project for those one-off clean-ups or catch-up jobs.

These aren't set in stone. Your real rate depends on your niche, where you live, what you offer and how confident you feel about your work.

Calculate Your Minimum Viable Rate

If you want to make sure you're not undercharging, start by figuring out how much you actually want to make. Say you need $3,000 a month. Next, think about how many hours you'll realistically bill—let's call it 60. Now, do the math: $3,000 divided by 60 hours gives you $50 an hour. That's your starting point. You can tweak it up or down later, depending on what works in your market or how you want to position yourself.

Think about offering **value-based packages**, too. Charging by the hour is simple, sure, but it can put a cap on what you earn. Packages, on the other hand, make things clearer for your clients and give you room to grow.

Here's how you might set it up:

Starter Package ($250/month): You handle basic transaction entry, bank reconciliation and monthly reports.

Growth Package ($450/month): Everything in Starter, plus invoicing, payroll support and quarterly reviews.

Premium Package ($750/month): The whole deal—full-service bookkeeping, advisory calls and tax prep coordination.

Packages help clients see exactly what they're paying for and you don't have to track every single minute. It's just a smoother way to work.

Be Transparent and Confident About Your Rates

When you quote your rates, just say it straight. There's no need to apologise or explain. Try something like, "*My standard rate for this service is...*" or "*This package is built for businesses like yours.*" Don't drop your price just because you feel nervous. Instead, throw in a little extra value, like a free onboarding call or a checklist. People pick up on your confidence. If you stand by your pricing, your clients usually will, too.

Keep checking in on your rates. The first numbers you set aren't permanent. As you get more experience, gather testimonials and work faster, take a fresh look at your prices every few months. Raise them bit by bit, let your clients know what's changing and always connect the price increase to something new you're offering.

Bottom line: Your starting rates are just that—a start, not a forever rule. Price your work so your business lasts, not just to scrape by. The more clients you serve, the more your value grows. Trust it.

What to Include (and Exclude) in Your Service Menu

Your service menu isn't just a bunch of options—it's your way of showing people what you do, who you're here for and how you make their lives better. Done correctly, it gives clients a clear picture of your services, lets them see what fits and helps them trust you from the start. When you're new to all this, it's so easy to go overboard with promises or, on the flip side, downplay what you can actually do.

What should you put on that first menu? And what should you skip?

Start with the basics. List the services your ideal client actually wants. Stick to things you know you can do well right now. Pick services that aren't just doable but are also easy for you to deliver every time—and make sure they actually turn a profit.

If you're putting together a beginner-friendly bookkeeping menu, here's what you'll want to include:

Monthly transaction categorization and reconciliation: This is your foundation. Every client needs someone to keep their books tidy each month.

Bank and credit card reconciliation: You'll catch mistakes early, and clients can trust their numbers.

Basic financial reports: Think monthly profit and loss, balance sheet and cash flow summaries. Clients love seeing where they stand.

Invoicing and bill entry: Keeps everything organized and cash flowing in the right direction.

Sales tax tracking (when needed): This one's huge for retail and service businesses. No one wants a surprise tax bill.

Catch-up or clean-up projects: Perfect for new clients who need to get their books in order, and a nice way to bring in extra income.

Client onboarding and setup: Make this a value-add or roll it into your first month's fee. Getting clients started on the right foot pays off.

Email support and monthly check-ins: Stay in touch, answer questions, and show clients you care.

One last thing: group these services into packages like Starter, Growth, or Premium. It makes pricing simpler — and scaling your business gets a whole lot easier.

What to Exclude (for Now)

Skip any services that:

- Demand skills you don't have yet

- Bring legal or regulatory headaches

- Eat up your time with little to show for it

- Mix bookkeeping with advisory or accounting work

When you're just starting out, leave these off your list:

Payroll processing: This stuff gets complicated fast—lots of compliance and every state has its own rules. Team up with a payroll provider if you need to.

Tax prep or filing: Unless you're actually licensed for this, steer clear. Bookkeeping doesn't cover taxes.

Financial forecasting or budgeting: That's an advisory role, not a beginner bookkeeping gig. Save it for later.

Inventory management for big businesses: If you get this wrong, it's a mess. Plus, it usually needs special software.

Custom software integrations or automation: If tech isn't your thing, these projects drain your energy and open the door to support issues.

Unlimited support or "all-you-can-eat" packages: Sounds nice, but you'll end up overworked and overwhelmed.

Bottom line: Only offer what you know you can handle right now. Start simple, focus on what you do well and let your service list grow along with your skills.

Finding Your First Clients

Chapter 3: The Warm Network Strategy

Mining Your Existing Connections Without Being Pushy

When you're just getting started, your best leads aren't random strangers—they're the people already in your corner. Friends, family, old coworkers, neighbors, even that person you chat with at the coffee shop.

They can point you in the right direction or connect you with someone who needs your skills. But let's be real: reaching out can feel awkward. No one wants to come across as pushy or desperate.

Here's the thing. It's not about pressure; it's about being curious, open and clear about what you do. Forget the whole "I need clients" mindset. Instead, focus on how you actually help—like, "I help small businesses get their finances in order so they can stress less." That shift changes everything. Suddenly, you're not begging for favours—you're showing people the value you bring.

Craft a Friendly Announcement

Just reach out with a quick, friendly note—something like:

"Hello [Name], I have some exciting news! I just launched my bookkeeping business. Right now, I'm working with small business owners who want to keep their finances organised and stress-free. If anyone comes to mind, send them my way—I'd love to chat."

Keep it easygoing and genuine. You're just letting them know what's new, not making a hard sell.

Make a List of Warm Contacts

Don't just stick to family. Think bigger. Who else do you know? Maybe old coworkers or managers. Other parents you chat with at school pickup or during your kid's soccer game. Local shop owners you've known for years. Friends who cut hair, fix cars or freelance. People from your church, gym or that community group you sometimes go to.

Try to list out 20 or 30 people. You're not asking them all for a job — you just want to start some conversations.

Go easy with your outreach. Skip the cold calls and blast emails. Instead, send a quick, personal DM or text. Invite someone out for coffee. Leave a real comment on their post — something that shows you're paying attention. Or share something useful on social media, like "3 signs your books need attention." Little things like these help people notice you and trust you and nobody feels pressured.

Offer a Low-Stakes Entry Point

Make it easy for people to say yes. Offer something simple—like a free 15-minute consultation, a handy checklist they can download or maybe a "first month half-price" deal if they come through a referral. These little things make it easier for people to take that first step.

Stay on their radar but don't be pushy. Most folks won't reply right away, and that's just how it goes. Keep sharing helpful tips, real success stories and the occasional reminder. When the time's right, they'll think of you.

Bottom line: Your network isn't just potential clients—it's filled with people who can open doors for you. Lead with generosity, not pressure. That's how you build real connections and find real opportunities.

The Announcement Post That Actually Converts

When people talk about an announcement post that actually converts, they mean a post—on social media or through email—that does more than just say, "Hey, I'm open for business." It gets people interested enough to reach out, book your services or refer you to someone else. Basically, it's not just about sharing news. It's about getting real action.

If you're a newly certified bookkeeper, you want your announcement post to do a few things really well:

First, be clear about your purpose. Don't just say, "I started a business." Instead, tell people exactly what you do, who you help and—this is key—how they can get in touch or support you.

Next, talk to the people who actually need you. Aim your message at small business owners, freelancers or anyone juggling a side hustle. Skip the vague stuff and get specific.

Finally, keep your language friendly and confident. Let your own voice come through but remain clear and professional. No need for jargon or stiff, formal phrases. You want people to feel like they know you—and trust you—right from the start.

Include a Call to Action

This part matters. A clear call to action points people in the right direction.

For example:

"Message me for a free consultation."

"Tag a friend who needs bookkeeping help."

"Check out my website to learn more."

Give people a reason to act.

Throw in something valuable, like:

A freebie — "Download my bookkeeping checklist for small businesses."

A limited-time deal — "First three clients get 25% off for three months."

Maybe a referral bonus — "Send someone my way and get a $50 gift card."

Here's an example email that's designed to convert readers into new clients:

Subject: I've Launched My Bookkeeping Business — Here's How You Can Help

Hello [First Name],

Big news—I've finally launched my own bookkeeping business and I'm officially open for new clients!

I work with small business owners, freelancers and service providers to keep everything organised and running smoothly. No more stressing over reconciliations, invoices or tax prep. I'll handle the numbers so you can get back to what you do best.

If you or anyone you know needs a bookkeeper you can actually count on, I'd love to chat. Right now, I'm offering:

- A free 15-minute consultation

- Flexible monthly packages built around what you need

- First-month discounts for new clients and referrals

You can get more info or book a call here: [Insert link]

Even if bookkeeping isn't on your radar at the moment, I'd really appreciate it if you kept me in mind or passed this along to someone who could use a hand.

Thanks a ton for your support—it honestly means everything as I dive into this new chapter!

Kind regards,

[First name] [Your Surname]

[Your Business Name]

[Your Website or Booking Link]

[Your Email Address]

[Optional: LinkedIn or social handle]

Asking for Referrals the Right Way

Referrals can seriously boost your bookkeeping business, especially when you're just starting out. When someone who trusts you introduces you to a new client, it's like skipping the awkward small talk and jumping right into business. Plus, these clients tend to stick around. The tough part? Actually asking for referrals. It feels weird if you don't know what to say.

The trick is to keep things simple, respectful and make sure everyone wins.

Here's why referrals work so well: people listen to people they trust. When someone vouches for you, you get instant credibility. That's tough to beat. Referrals bring in better clients, speed up the whole sales process and help you spend less on marketing. And those clients? They usually stay longer.

Don't assume referrals will just fall into your lap. Sometimes you have to ask for them—and you want to do it the right way.

How to Ask Without Feeling Pushy

Here's an easy, low-key way to ask:

"I'm building up my bookkeeping business and looking for a few new clients. If you happen to know any small business owners or freelancers who need help keeping their finances in order, I'd really appreciate a referral. No pressure — just wanted to mention it."

Why does this work? It's relaxed, feels like a real conversation and it's all about helping people. You're not pushing anyone to make a sale for you. You're just letting them know how they can help if they want.

When should you ask? Timing is everything. The best moments are:

- Right after you wrap up a project that went well
- When a client thanks you or says he's happy
- During a regular check-in or review call
- In a follow-up email after you've delivered good results

You can also drop a quick referral note in your email signature or your onboarding materials. It's an easy way to keep the idea out there.

Sweeten the Deal (Optional)

You don't have to offer an incentive but **a small reward** can give people a little nudge. Maybe it's a gift card or a discount for every referral or a free month of service after three. Even a simple thank-you note or a surprise can go a long way. The point isn't to buy loyalty—it's just about saying thanks.

Make sharing as easy as possible. Give people something they can copy and send, like a quick blurb or a link to your site or booking page. Maybe offer a downloadable flyer or a handy checklist. Even a ready-made referral form or email template helps. The less effort it takes, the more likely they'll actually refer you.

Here's what matters: referrals don't have to feel weird if you treat them as a way to help others. Ask with confidence, show your appreciation and make it simple for people to connect you with those who can use your help.

Chapter 4: Local Business Outreach

Identifying Businesses in Your Area That Need Bookkeepers

You don't need fancy marketing to land your first clients. Honestly, it's more about paying attention—spotting the local businesses that look a little lost with their books. A lot of small business owners are swamped, buried under receipts or just don't realise how much easier life gets when you have a bookkeeper. Your job? Find them and show them you can help.

Look for businesses where cash flow matters day-to-day. These folks deal with piles of transactions, run payroll, pay contractors or have to keep track of every expense when tax time rolls around. The usual suspects? Think restaurants and coffee shops, hair salons and barbers, plumbers, electricians, landscapers, small retail stores, fitness trainers, designers, photographers, writers, even childcare providers and mobile mechanics.

Most don't have an in-house finance person, and plenty are behind on reconciliations, tax prep or invoicing. That's where you come in.

Use Local Directories and Listings

If you're looking for businesses nearby, start by searching **Google Maps** or **Yelp**—just type in what you need, like "plumbers near me." Your local Chamber of Commerce or small business group usually has a directory too, so don't skip that.

Facebook's packed with business pages and neighborhood groups where people share recommendations. **Craigslist Services** and **Thumbtack** list a bunch of providers who are working in your area right now. Also, farmers' markets, craft fairs and pop-up events are goldmines for finding small-business owners. As you go, jot down any businesses that are clearly active but might not have their finances totally set up yet.

Look for Signs That They Might Need Help

Once you spot some businesses that look like a good fit, pay attention to the little things. Maybe their website lists an old phone number or there's no mention of bookkeeping anywhere. If you see reviews where people complain about messy billing or bad organization, that's another hint.

Sometimes you'll notice social media posts where the owner admits they're drowning in paperwork or just can't keep up. **Seasonal businesses**, especially right before their busy times, often show signs they're overwhelmed. Stuff like this usually means they could use a hand—especially if you reach out in a way that feels real and understanding.

Now, when you're ready to connect, don't go in with a generic pitch. Try something like:

"Hello [Name], I found your business and would like to introduce myself. I'm a local bookkeeper who helps small businesses stay on top of their finances and avoid stress. If you ever need some help with your books—or even just want to talk through your options—I'd love to chat."

Keep it casual, friendly and make it clear you're just here to help, not sell. Your next client could be right around the corner. Pay attention, do your research and reach out with confidence. Most local business owners really appreciate support from someone who actually gets what they're dealing with.

Partnership Opportunities with CPAs, Business Consultants and Attorneys

You don't have to build your client list all by yourself. Think about it: CPAs, business consultants and attorneys already have relationships with the exact people who need bookkeeping. Happily, they're usually on the lookout for reliable folks to refer.

If you show up as a trustworthy, easy-to-work-with bookkeeper, you can plug right into their networks. These partnerships really pay off in the long run.

Here's why this works. These pros:

- Work with business owners who want financial clarity.

- Usually don't handle the day-to-day bookkeeping themselves.
- Like their clients to be organized and follow the rules.
- Really appreciate specialists who make their lives easier.

When you help their clients keep their books in order, everyone comes out ahead — including you.

CPAs: Your Tax Season Allies

CPAs hate dealing with a pile of messy books at the end of the year. If you team up with a bookkeeper who keeps everything organized and up to date, you save time and cut down on mistakes.

Here's how to reach out to CPAs:

- Offer to handle monthly reconciliations and sort out transactions for their clients.
- Let them know you're basically their right-hand person—someone who makes tax season way less stressful.
- See if they'd be willing to refer clients who need steady, reliable support.
- Share a sample report or walk them through your workflow so they get a sense of your professionalism.

Business consultants are another great group to connect with. They're all about helping companies grow and run better but, to do that, they need solid financial data. That's where you step in.

How to approach consultants:

Let them know you'll keep their clients' books clean and handle regular reports so they can focus on strategy. Show how your work fits right alongside their big-picture advice. Mention the idea of teaming up—maybe through referrals or even bundled services. And don't just sit behind a desk; show up at local business events or webinars where consultants hang out.

Attorneys—especially those in small firms or working solo—help business owners set up LLCs, draft contracts and keep things compliant. But here's the thing: after all that legal work, someone still has to handle the books. That's usually not them.

Reach out to those attorneys. Focus on the ones helping entrepreneurs. Offer to take care of their clients once the paperwork is done—handle the financial setup and tracking. Bring a simple flyer or checklist that they can give to new business owners. Make it clear you're there to help, not compete.

How to Start the Conversation

Hello [Name], I'm a local bookkeeper and work a lot with small businesses and freelancers. I've noticed my clients do better when they have a solid team behind them so I'm reaching out to connect. Maybe we can find ways to help each others' clients grow. Want to grab a quick call and chat?

When you connect, make sure you give first. Send referrals their way, share useful templates or resources, offer a free consultation for their clients or even team up for a webinar. Real partnerships start with generosity and showing up when it counts.

Bottom line: The right partnerships can bring in steady referrals and boost your reputation. CPAs, consultants and attorneys are often the ones who send the best clients your way. Show them you're the bookkeeper they've been looking for.

Chapter 5: Digital Prospecting Methods

Digital Prospecting Methods

These days, if you want to find new bookkeeping clients, digital prospecting just makes sense—especially when you're starting out. You don't have to rely on who you already know. You can show off what you do, reach a much bigger crowd and pick up leads without even leaving your house.

Here's how you can use the internet to find clients (and actually look like you know what you're doing while you're at it):

1. Make Your LinkedIn Stand Out

LinkedIn can be a serious game-changer - but only if you use it correctly.

Start by fixing up your headline. Say something clear, like "Helping small businesses stay financially organised | Freelance Bookkeeper." Next, write a summary that spells out who you help, how you work and what sets you apart from the crowd.

Don't just sit back—connect with local business owners, freelancers and others in your field. Get involved. Leave comments, share your perspective or offer a quick tip when you see a post that fits your expertise. It's a good idea to post your own stuff, too—bookkeeping advice, stories about your clients' wins (with permission) or even a peek at how you work behind the scenes.

Quick tip: LinkedIn has search filters so you can zero in on people by industry, location or job title. Use them, and when you reach out, make your connection request personal. No one likes a generic message.

2. Join Facebook Groups and Online Communities

Lots of small business owners hang out in Facebook groups, Reddit threads and other online forums to swap advice and ask questions. Try searching for groups like "Small Business Owners USA", "Freelancers & Creatives" or "Startup Support".

When you join, focus on helping out—answer questions, share helpful resources and build some real trust. If it fits the conversation, mention what you do or offer a free consultation.

Keep an eye out for posts where people talk about money stress, tax headaches or feeling disorganized. That's your moment to jump in and help. Here's an extra tip: think about starting your own group focused on financial clarity for small businesses.

3. Use Email Outreach (Warm and Cold)

Email works. It's still one of the best ways to kick off real conversations. Start with warm leads: people you've met, chatted with or who already follow you somewhere. Keep your message short and friendly. Just say who you are, what you do and ask if they're up for a quick chat.

Going in cold? Do a little homework first. Find out what the business actually does and mention something specific in your message. Make it personal, not spammy.

Always end with a clear question, like, "Want to hop on a quick call next week?" And if you need help finding real email addresses, tools like Hunter.io or Apollo make it way easier to track down the right people at small businesses.

4. Leverage Freelance Platforms

Sites like **Upwork, Fiverr** and **Thumbtack** are great for landing those first clients and showing people what you can do. Set up a sharp profile and make sure your services are clear—think keywords like "monthly bookkeeping", "QuickBooks clean-up" or "Xero support." Jump onto job postings fast and always tweak your proposals to fit what the client needs.

When you finish a project, ask happy clients to leave a review—good feedback will help you stand out. Just remember, these sites are crowded. They're good for getting started but don't plan to stick around there forever.

5. Create Lead Magnets and Landing Pages

A **lead magnet** is just a free resource you offer (like a free eBook) to draw in potential clients —basically, you give them something useful, like a "Bookkeeping Checklist for Freelancers", "5 Signs Your Books Need Help" or a "Tax Prep Starter Guide" and in return, they share their email with you.

Share your lead magnet everywhere you can: on social media, in online groups or through email. Set up a straightforward **landing page with a sign-up form** to collect these leads and offer a free consultation to get the ball rolling.

This approach helps you grow your email list and shows people you actually know your stuff.

Digital prospecting is about showing up where your ideal clients already hang out, offering something valuable and starting real conversations. When you do this consistently and keep your message clear, your online presence turns into your best lead generator, hands down.

Facebook groups where small business owners congregate

Facebook groups are one of the best places to connect with small business owners, especially if you show up ready to help instead of just selling. You get direct access to your ideal clients and you can actually talk to them in real time.

If you want to meet new people, understand what they're struggling with and build trust before you ever mention your services, these groups make it easy. Entrepreneurs are always posting questions, talking about what's difficult for them and looking for advice. That's your chance to jump in and show you know your stuff.

How to Find the Right Groups

Look for active groups where people post regularly, have discussions and leave comments.

Visit Facebook and try searching for things like "Small Business Owners USA", "Freelancers and Entrepreneurs", "Startup Support" or even "Women in Business". You can get more specific with "Local Business Network" and your city or state or go for groups like "Creative Entrepreneurs" or "Service-Based Business Owners".

When you check out these groups, pay attention to a few things. Are people actually posting and talking or does it feel like a ghost town? Look at the rules—especially the ones concerning product or service promotion. Some groups are really strict about self-promotion. Also, see who the group's for. Is it mostly U.S. small businesses, solo founders or a certain industry? That way, you know if you're in the right spot.

Recommended Groups (2025)

Based on current listings on radianmarketing.com[1], Gusto[2] and TheMktgBoy[3], here are a few standout groups worth exploring:

Group Name	Focus Area	Members
Small Business Owners Community	General support & networking	100
Freelance & Service-Based Entrepreneurs	Freelancers, consultants, creatives	50K+
Women Helping Women Entrepreneurs	Female-led businesses	600K+
Startup Business Advice & Networking	Early-stage founders & startups	80K+
Local Business Owners (your city)	City-specific networking	(Varies)

When you join, **focus on earning trust.** Jump in and answer questions—especially ones about bookkeeping, getting finances organized or tax prep. Share useful stuff like checklists, templates or quick videos that actually help people out. When you comment, show some empathy and offer real advice, not just links or sales pitches.

Introduce yourself in a way that highlights how you help, like, "I help small businesses stay financially organized—ask me anything!" And don't spam or

1. https://radianmarketing.com/top-facebook-groups-for-business-owners/

2. https://gusto.com/resources/articles/business-growth/tech-tools/best-facebook-groups-entrepreneurs

3. https://themktgboy.com/facebook-groups-for-small-business/

drop random links unless someone asks for them. You want people to see you as a helpful person, not just another ad.

When to Mention Your Services

Keep an eye out for posts where people mention **financial stress**, tax headaches or feeling disorganized. Maybe someone's asking about bookkeeping tools or how to handle invoicing. Or they drop a line like, "I'm behind on my books" or "Admin work drives me crazy". That's your cue.

Jump in with some genuine empathy. Say something like, "I help small businesses with this stuff all the time—happy to chat if you ever need a hand". Keep it friendly, no pressure.

Bottom line? Facebook groups are packed with the kind of clients you want. Just show up, actually help and let people see what you know. Skip the hard sell. Join groups that make sense, be genuine and let your expertise do the talking.

LinkedIn Outreach That Doesn't Feel Salesy

LinkedIn gives you a real shot at connecting with small business owners, freelancers and professionals who actually need bookkeeping help. But let's be honest—if your first message feels like a sales pitch, most people won't even bother to reply. Here's the thing: *people respond to value, not a hard sell.*

Now, how do you actually **make real connections** without coming off as pushy? Start by shifting your focus. Don't show up thinking, "How do I land a new client?" Instead, try, "How can I genuinely help this person move forward?" Once you flip that switch, everything changes. The whole conversation feels natural—like you're just two people talking, not a salesperson chasing a quota.

Craft a Friendly, Personalised Message

Skip the bland intros. Make your message about them—their job, their field, or something they've done lately.

For instance:

"Hello [Name], I saw that you run a creative agency. That's really cool. I help small businesses stay on top of their finances so things run smoother and with less stress. If you ever want a hand with your bookkeeping or just want to swap ideas, let's chat."

Why does this land well?

It feels personal.

It offers help, not a sales pitch.

It's relaxed and sure of itself.

Connect First, Then Reach Out

Don't just send a cold message. Take a minute to engage—"like" or comment on their posts, share something helpful or point out something you genuinely appreciate about their work. This way, when you finally reach out, it feels less awkward and a lot more genuine.

Give Before You Get

Skip the sales pitch. Offer something useful instead. Maybe it's a free checklist, a quick industry tip (like "3 bookkeeping mistakes creatives make"), or an invitation to a no-strings Q&A. When you lead with real value, you come across as someone who wants to help, not just another person trying to sell something.

Follow Up Respectfully

If you don't hear back, give it a week or two, then send a friendly follow-up:

"Hello [Name], just checking in—maybe my last message got lost. If you ever want to talk about bookkeeping or need some financial clarity, I'm around."

No pressure, no hard sell. Just a quick reminder that you're here if they need anything.

Bottom line: LinkedIn works best when you treat it like a real conversation, not a sales pitch. Be curious, be helpful and let your knowledge do the talking.

Online Business Communities and Forums

Step away from the noise of social media and you'll find a whole world of online communities where small business owners actually talk, swap stories and help each other out. These forums feel more quiet than Facebook or LinkedIn but really, that's what makes them so valuable. Real conversations happen there. You get a shot at real connections, insider info and, if you play your cards correctly, new clients, too.

When you jump in with useful advice and a willingness to help, people will start to notice. Before long, you'll be the bookkeeper everyone trusts—right in the middle of the places your dream clients already spend their time.

Where to Find These Communities

Here are some popular platforms and forums where U.S.-based entrepreneurs and small business owners hang out:

Platform/Forum	Focus Area	Why It's Useful
Reddit (r/smallbusiness, r/entrepreneur)	Broad business advice & peer support	Active discussions, anonymous questions
Alignable	Local business networking	Connects you with nearby business owners
Indie Hackers	Startups, freelancers, solopreneurs	Great for tech-savvy and online-first clients
Quora	Q & A across industries	Answer bookkeeping questions to build authority
Warrior Forum	Online marketing & small business	Ideal for service-based entrepreneurs
Startups.com Community	Early-stage founders & freelancers	Focused on growth and systems

How to Engage Effectively

If you want people to trust you and notice your work, jump in and answer questions—especially when it comes to bookkeeping, invoicing or just staying organized with finances. Don't just talk about what you do; actually share what you've learned and what's worked for you, without making it sound like a sales pitch.

When you post, use a signature that's simple and clear, like "Peter | Freelance Bookkeeper for Small Businesses | [Website]." Get involved in conversations—start new threads or ask questions that get people talking. Don't push your services unless someone asks. Most forums are strict about self-promotion so play it cool.

What to Watch For

Keep an eye out for posts like these:

"I'm behind on my books—what do I do?"

"How do I get ready for tax season as a freelancer?"

"What bookkeeping software works best for small businesses?"

"I'm lost when it comes to organizing my finances—have any advice?"

This is your chance to step in, share some helpful advice and naturally mention what you offer.

Build a Profile That Shows You Know Your Stuff

Most forums let you set up a profile. Don't let that space go to waste. Share a bit about your background and your niche, drop a link to your website or a useful resource and show your expertise without sounding like you're bragging. Even if you're not posting every day, your profile still puts you on the radar.

Bottom line: Online business communities are packed with people who need what you offer. Show up, be generous, keep things clear and stick around. Treat these places like real conversations—not marketing blasts—and you'll start building relationships that actually turn into clients.

Using Upwork or Fiverr the Smart Way

Upwork and Fiverr can open doors when you're just starting out with bookkeeping clients but you have to be smart about it. These sites move fast, everyone's competing for attention and some people will want the lowest price possible. Don't get too comfortable—think of these platforms as launch pads, not places to settle down for good.

Let's break down how to use them to your advantage—and what you should watch for:

How the Platforms Work

Upwork is all about projects and hourly gigs. Clients post jobs, you send in proposals. It's better for building longer-term relationships or landing recurring work.

Fiverr works the other way around. You set up your services as "gigs", then clients buy straight from your page. It's more about one-off tasks or packaged services.

Each gives you a shot at global clients, some level of payment protection and a place to show off your skills. However, there are fees, *lots* of competition and a few hoops to jump through.

Why You'd Want to Use Them

- You get your name in front of real buyers quickly.
- Reviews and ratings help you build trust, even if you're new.
- Payments are secure. If there's an issue, there's a process to sort it out.
- Easy way to build up your portfolio.
- You don't need a fancy website or ads to get started.

These sites work well if you want to:

- Test out your pricing and see what sticks.
- Build confidence and rack up some experience.

- Collect testimonials and feedback for later.
- Fill in the gaps while you're working on your own client list.

What to Watch Out For

- Competition is *fierce* and there's always pressure to drop your prices.
- Platform fees can take 10–20% of what you earn.
- You don't really control the client relationship—the platform does.
- Scope creep is real. Sometimes you'll get clients who ask for more than you agreed to.
- Writing proposals (especially on Upwork) can eat up a lot of time.

If you're not careful, it's easy to get stuck chasing low-paying gigs, working too much for too little and missing out on better opportunities elsewhere.

How to Really Win on Freelance Platforms

- Get specific with your services. Don't just offer "bookkeeping"—try something like "Monthly bookkeeping for Etsy sellers" or "QuickBooks clean-up for freelancers". The more tailored your offer, the better.
- Show off your work. On sites like Fiverr, your visuals and descriptions matter—a lot. Make them stand out.
- When someone messages you, get back to him fast and keep it clear. Clients love quick, professional responses.
- After you finish a project, ask for a review. Positive feedback pushes you up in the rankings and makes you look trustworthy.

- Keep an eye on your time and what you're actually earning. If a gig isn't worth it, move on.

- As you rack up experience, don't just leave it sitting on the platform. Add those wins to your website or LinkedIn. Use that credibility everywhere.

Think of Upwork and Fiverr as launchpads, not your end goal. Use them to get momentum, sharpen your pitch and build some confidence. But don't settle. Once you have a few good stories under your belt, start reaching out for referrals, build partnerships and do your own outreach. That's where the real growth happens.

Bottom line: Freelance platforms are a great way to start, as long as you're intentional about how you use them. Focus on quality, not just cranking out jobs. Treat every gig as a step toward landing the clients you actually want.

Converting Prospects into Clients

Chapter 6: Initial Conversations

The Discovery Call Framework

A discovery call isn't a sales pitch. It's a real conversation. This is your chance to get to know what the client actually needs, start building trust, and figure out if you two are a good match. When you do it correctly, you set the stage for a solid working relationship. Onboarding will feel easy and smooth.

If you're new to talking with clients, here's a straightforward framework you can use for every discovery call:

Step 1: Start Warm

Kick things off with a friendly vibe. Thank him/her for showing up and keep things relaxed but professional. Maybe say something like, "Thanks for making time today. I'm looking forward to hearing about your business and seeing how I can help". Don't dive straight into business. Ask a simple question to break the ice, like, "How's your week going?" or "What's your day-to-day work like?" It helps everyone relax and makes the conversation flow better.

Step 2: Get to Know Their Business

Ask open questions so you can really understand how things work on their end. Try, "Can you walk me through your business and how it's set up?" or "What systems do you use for bookkeeping or invoicing?" and "Is anyone helping with your finances now?" Listen closely. Take notes. Pay attention to where they're struggling or where there might be room for improvement.

Step 3: Dig Into Their Challenges

Now, find out what's not working for them. Ask things like, "What's the most frustrating part of handling your books?" or "Are there deadlines or is there compliance stuff that worries you?" or "Do you feel confident about your financial reports and tax prep?" This is where you get to the real reasons why they reached out—and it's your opening to show how you can help.

Step 4: Explain How You Can Help

Once you have the full picture, share how your services fit their needs. For example, "From what you've told me, I'd suggest starting with monthly reconciliations, basic reporting and cleaning up your records. That'll give you clarity and peace of mind when tax time rolls around". Keep it simple. Talk about the results, not just features.

Step 5: Cover the Basics (Briefly)

If things are going well, you can touch on how you work—your process, how you communicate, usual turnaround times and how your pricing or packages work. Mention next steps if they're interested. No pressure here. You're guiding, not pushing for a sale.

Step 6: Open the Floor and Wrap Up

Invite any questions. Maybe say, "Is there anything you're wondering about?" or "Would you like me to send over a proposal or engagement letter to look at?" Thank him again and let him know what's next—whether that's a follow-up email, a quote or just when he can expect to hear from you.

Bottom line: A great discovery call is all about listening. When you show real curiosity and keep things clear, you build trust. That's what brings clients in.

Digging Into Real Pain Points

When clients come to you, they're rarely just looking for help with a to-do list. Usually, there's something deeper—a frustration, a fear or a nagging problem that just won't go away. That's what keeps them up at night. Your real job, especially in those first conversations, is to gently get to the heart of what's really bothering them. That way, you can show them how your services actually solve their real problems.

How do you do it? You ask the right questions and actually listen—not just to their words, but to what's underneath.

Why You Need to Know Their Pain Points

Once you know what's really going on, everything gets easier. You can:

- Shape your offer around what they truly need
- Build real trust because you understand
- Explain your pricing without awkwardness, since the value is clear
- Create genuine urgency—no hard selling needed

Pain points aren't just problems; they're triggers. Get to the emotional root and you'll help clients make confident choices.

Smart Questions That Go Deeper

Don't just ask about bookkeeping tasks. Use questions that dig into their workflow, worries and goals:

Business Clarity & Organization

How do you keep track of your income and expenses right now?

Are you confident in your financial reports each month?

What's your routine for getting ready for tax season?

Time & Efficiency

How many hours a week do you spend on admin or bookkeeping?

Is managing your books eating into time you'd rather spend elsewhere?

Do you ever miss a deadline or just feel buried under paperwork?

Financial Stress & Risk

Ever been hit with an unexpected tax bill or cash flow issue?

Are you worried about making mistakes that'll cost you?

Do you feel in control of your finances or are you mostly reacting to problems?

Growth & Goals

Are you planning to grow or scale your business this year?

Do you already have financial systems to support that growth?

What would it mean if your books were always up to date?

Listen for the Real Stuff

Sometimes clients just come out and say it:

"I hate doing this stuff."

"I'm always behind."

"I just want to focus on my actual work."

"I'm worried I'll mess something up."

These aren't just complaints—they're clues. They show you exactly where you can help.

Show That You Get It

When you spot a pain point, say it back to them. For example:

"It sounds like bookkeeping eats up a lot of your time and adds stress during tax season. That's exactly what I help with so you can focus on growing your business and feel at ease."

That's how clients know you understand, and that you're ready to help.

Bottom Line: Pain points aren't always obvious. Ask open-ended questions, pay close attention and respond with empathy. When clients feel truly heard, saying "yes" comes naturally.

Listening for Buying Signals

Most clients won't come right out and say, "I'm ready to hire you". Instead, they'll drop hints—if you're paying attention. Buying signals are little things people say or do that show they're moving closer to a decision. When you catch them, you can step up, steer the conversation and help things move forward naturally.

What do these signals sound like? Here's how to spot them during calls, chats or even online messages:

Common Verbal Buying Signals

When someone says things like:

"How soon could we get started?"

"What would the next step look like?"

"Do you work with businesses like mine?"

"I've been meaning to get help with this."

"That sounds exactly like what I need."

"I'm not great with numbers—I could really use support."

They aren't just making small talk. These are invitations. That's your cue to shift gears from just chatting to actually helping them take action.

Behavioral Buying Signals

Even if a prospective client doesn't say anything direct, you can still pick up on interest by what he or she does. Watch for things like:

- Asking specific questions about your process or pricing
- Opening up about his/her business challenges
- Getting involved in the conversation—nodding, taking notes, leaning in
- Replying to your emails or messages quickly
- Checking out your website or downloading your resources

- Referring other people to you before he's even signed up himself

These signs usually mean they trust you and want to know more—big steps toward saying yes.

How to Respond to Buying Signals

The moment you spot a buying signal, don't slam on the sales pitch. Ease into it. You might say:

"Sounds like this has been on your mind for a while—want me to walk you through how we'd get started?"

Or:

"I can send over a proposal with a few package options—would that help?"

Keep it relaxed and collaborative, not pushy.

What to Avoid

Don't get so caught up in your own script that you miss what your client is telling you.

Don't drown him in technical talk or try to upsell everything at once.

Don't pressure him into a decision if he's not ready.

Don't sit around waiting for a formal "yes" while all the buying signals pass you by.

Buying signals can be subtle but they're powerful. Miss them, and you might miss the whole opportunity.

Key Takeaway: Clients almost never say, "I'm ready" straight out. So listen for the clues, respond confidently and make it easy for them to take the next step. Meet their interest with some clarity and things should just fall into place.

When to Talk About Price

Figuring out when to bring up pricing is always a bit tricky. If you mention it too soon, it feels cold and transactional. Too late, you might risk confusion or mismatched expectations. The sweet spot is after you've built trust and made the value clear—but before the client leaves the conversation still wondering what it's going to cost.

Here's how to get the timing right:

Don't Lead with Price—Lead with Value

If you open with your rates, clients start judging you by cost alone. Instead, start by:

- Really understanding their business and what's bugging them
- Showing how your services solve their specific problems
- Explaining your process and why people trust you

Once they see the value, talking about price feels natural, not like a barrier.

Look for Natural Openings

Clients will usually give you a cue when they're ready to talk numbers. Listen for things like:

"How does your service work?"

"What would something like that cost?"

"Do you offer packages or hourly rates?"

"What's the next step if I want to move forward?"

These are green lights. At this point, you can talk pricing with confidence.

How to Introduce Pricing Smoothly

When it feels right, just be straightforward and calm:

"Based on what you've shared, I'd recommend starting with my Starter Package. It includes monthly reconciliations and basic reporting for $300/month - and it's built for businesses like yours."

Or:

"I offer flexible packages depending on what you need. Want me to walk you through a few options?"

This way, you're guiding—not selling.

When Not to Talk About Price

Skip the pricing talk if:

- It's your very first message or cold outreach
- You don't understand the client's scope or needs yet
- The client seems unsure or overwhelmed
- You're still figuring out what services they actually want

Jumping to price too soon kills trust and makes the whole thing feel rushed.

Key Takeaway:

Talk about price only after you've built some context and shown your value. When clients understand what they're getting, they're much more likely to accept the cost—and move ahead without hesitation.

Chapter 7: Proposals That Win

Bookkeeping Proposal Template

[Your Business Name]

[Your Name]

[Email Address] | [Phone Number] | [Website]

Date: [Insert date]

Client: [Client's Name]

Business: [Client's Business Name]

Contact: [Client's Email and/or Phone]

1. Overview

Thanks for considering [Your Business Name] for your bookkeeping. After chatting with you, I've put together this proposal. It spells out the services I recommend, the pricing and what comes next so you'll know exactly what to expect. My goal is to keep your finances organised and make things less stressful for you.

2. Scope of Services

Here's what I'll handle for you:

- Categorising and reconciling transactions each month

- Bank and credit card reconciliation

- Basic financial reports (Profit & Loss, Balance Sheet)

- Invoicing and entering bills

- Email support and a monthly check-in

Want something extra? We can add things like catch-up work or sales tax tracking, no problem.

3. Pricing

Starter Package – $300/month

Covers up to 100 transactions, monthly reports and basic support

Growth Package – $450/month

Covers up to 200 transactions, adds invoicing, quarterly reviews and priority support

Custom Package – [Insert price]

I'll build a plan around your business, based on what you need

One-time clean-up projects are priced separately.

4. Timeline & Onboarding

Once you accept this proposal and finish a few onboarding forms, I'll get started. Onboarding usually takes 3–5 business days. Here's what happens:

- I'll set up secure access (like QuickBooks and bank feeds)

- Do an initial review of your current records

- Check in at the end of the first month and make any needed adjustments

5. Terms & Payment

You'll get your invoice on the 1st of each month.

Please pay within 7 days using [preferred method].

You can pause or end our agreement any time with 14 days' notice.

6. Next Steps

Ready to get going?

1. Just reply to this email and say you're in

2. I'll send you a formal engagement letter and onboarding checklist

3. We'll set up your onboarding call and jump in

Looking forward to working together,

[Name] [Your Surname]

[Your Business Name]

[Your Contact Info]

Key Takeaway: A clear, straightforward proposal makes it easy for clients to say yes. Focus on value, keep things simple and make the next steps obvious.

Handling the "I Found Someone Cheaper" Objection

Sooner or later, you'll hear it: "I found someone cheaper". It stings a bit, especially when you're new. Of course, cheap doesn't always mean better. This is your chance to show why you're worth it.

You're not here to race to the bottom on price. You're here to show your value.

What's really going on when someone brings up cost? **There's usually more to it than just the price tag.** Maybe they're watching their budget. Maybe they don't see what sets you apart—yet. Sometimes they're nervous about outsourcing or just comparing options before making a decision.

Don't get defensive. Get clear.

How to Respond (and Keep Your Confidence)

Try something like this:

"I get it, there are plenty of choices out there. My focus is on giving you reliable, personalised support—helping you stay organised and confident about your finances. I might not be the cheapest but I work hard to be the most dependable and the easiest to work with."

Or you could say:

"Lower prices often mean less support, rushed work or surprise costs later. I'm upfront about pricing, keep communication clear and double down on accuracy so you actually save time and stress in the end."

Shift the conversation. Make it about value, trust and results.

Show What Makes You Different

This is your moment to shine a light on your strengths:

- Monthly reports and reconciliations you can actually understand

- Fast responses and genuine care for your business

- Packages you can customize to fit your needs

- Books that are clean and audit-ready, saving you time and money

- No mystery fees, no confusing invoices

If you offer onboarding help, regular check-ins, or educational resources, mention those—they make a real difference and people notice.

Lower the Risk

Still feeling some hesitation from the client? Offer a way in without a big commitment:

- One-time clean-up projects

- A discounted first month

- Free consultations or audits

- Starter packages with a clear, limited scope

Let them try you out. Most of the time, that's all it takes for them to see the value and stick around.

Bottom line: When someone brings up a cheaper competitor, don't freak out. Pivot and focus on the real value and peace of mind you bring to the table. The right clients will get it.

Building Trust When You Lack Testimonials

Starting out without any testimonials? Yeah, it can feel like a big roadblock. Yet, trust isn't just about reviews. It's about how you show up for people. Clients want more than just a service — they're looking for confidence, clarity and a real connection. If you can bring those to the table, you'll land work, even if no one's reviewed you yet.

Here's how you can build trust right from the start:

People trust what makes sense. **Make everything about your business easy to understand** — your services, your pricing, your process. Spell things out in plain English. Walk clients through what happens when they sign up, step by step.

Show off **sample reports or dashboards** so people get a taste of what you actually do. Be upfront about how long things take, how you'll communicate and what you'll deliver. When you're clear, people feel more confident. That's the foundation of trust.

Show, don't just tell.

No testimonials? Let your work do the talking. Put together a **sample case study**. It doesn't even have to be real, just realistic. Show a "before and after" scenario to highlight the difference you make. Offer a free guide or checklist to prove you know your stuff.

Share helpful tips on LinkedIn or in Facebook groups to get your name out there. All of this shows people you're an expert they can rely on, not just another faceless service.

Use social proof in other ways.

Testimonials aren't the only way to show people you're legit. Mention any **training, certifications or software skills** you have. Tell your story, especially if you have small business experience yourself. If you have reviews from places like Upwork or Fiverr, share those. Even positive feedback from peers or mentors counts. Sometimes a kind word from a colleague goes a long way.

Offer a low-risk first step.

Make it easy for clients to dip their toes in. Maybe offer a one-time clean-up project, a discounted first month or a satisfaction guarantee. Let people pause or cancel any time. A free, no-strings-attached consultation works, too. Lowering the risk gives clients a chance to see your value for themselves.

Be human, not perfect.

People want to work with real humans, not robots. Be warm, honest and actually listen. Follow up when you say you will. Ask good questions. Listen more than you talk. If you don't know something, admit it — and share how you keep learning. Being real builds trust way faster than trying to be flawless.

Bottom line? You don't need a pile of testimonials to earn trust. You just need to be clear, consistent and genuinely want to help. Show up, deliver value and act with integrity. The testimonials will come.

How to Follow Up Without Being Annoying

You have to follow up. That's just the way it goes. Still, incorrectly done, you might sound like a robot. Worse, you'll come off as pushy. The point isn't to chase anyone—it's to offer a quick reminder, re-spark the conversation and actually be useful. Great follow-ups show you respect their time, build trust and keep things friendly without ever making people feel cornered.

Here's the right way to do it—no pestering, just real connection:

Why Good Follow-Ups Work

People forget things. They get sidetracked. Sometimes they just need a little more time. When you follow up thoughtfully, you show you're professional and dependable. You stay on their radar. You help clear up any confusion. You remind them they're worth talking to - without making them sit through your pitch all over again. It's not about "checking in"; it's about being genuinely helpful.

A Simple 3-Step Follow-Up Plan

Here's a straightforward sequence you can use for pretty much anything—discovery calls, proposals, email inquiries, you name it:

Day 2: Friendly Nudge

"Hello [Name], just wanted to thank you again for our chat the other day. If you have any questions or need more info about the proposal, I'm here."

Keep it light, short and leave the door open.

Day 5–7: Share Something Useful

"Hi [Name], thought you might like this—a checklist I use with new clients to stay organized during tax season. Let me know if you want to talk more about the proposal."

Now you've given them something they can actually use and you look like a resource, not a salesperson.

Day 10–14: Wrap Up, But Don't Slam the Door

"Hello [Name], I'll close the loop here for now but if you need any help with your books down the road, I'm always here. Wishing you the best with your business!"

You've ended things on a good note but you've left the door open in case they want to come back.

How to Keep Your Follow-Ups From Being Annoying

- Don't crowd their inbox—space out your emails.

- Mix things up—don't just send the same message over and over.

- Always offer something useful—a tip, checklist or resource goes a long way.

- Use clear, honest subject lines like "Quick follow-up", "Resource for your books" or "Closing the loop."

- Make it easy to answer—ask a yes/no question or drop a simple link to book a call.

What You Should Avoid

- Don't send a "Just checking in..." email with no real context.

- Don't guilt-trip or pressure them.

- Skip the stuffy, robotic language.

- Nobody wants to read a long, rambling email with no clear point.

- Don't follow up too often or without adding anything new.

Ask yourself—would I want this in my inbox? If not, don't send it.

Bottom Line: Follow-ups shouldn't feel like sales pressure—they should feel like gentle reminders. If you lead with respect and real value, people will remember you. When they're ready, they'll come back.

Chapter 8: Closing Your First Clients

Getting Past "I Need to Think About It"

You've just finished a solid discovery call. The client seems interested, you've laid out your services and things are going well. Then comes the pause: "I need to think about it." It's a classic move. Honestly, it doesn't mean "no." Usually, they're just weighing things over, making comparisons, or maybe they're a little hesitant. Your job is to meet them with empathy, keep things clear and give them a gentle nudge—not a shove.

Here's how to handle it confidently and without coming off as pushy:

First, try to get where they're coming from. When someone says he needs time, it's often because he's:

- Looking at other options or prices.

- Unsure about making a commitment.

- Feeling a bit overwhelmed or distracted.

- Waiting on input from a partner or his team.

- Nervous about handing something sensitive to someone new.

Your answer should make him feel comfortable and informed, never rushed.

What do you actually say? Something like:

"Of course, I want you to feel good about your decision. If it helps, I can send a quick summary of what we talked about, plus a few package options and next steps. That way, you'll have everything in front of you when you're ready."

This keeps things professional and leaves the door open.

A few days later, check in—gently:

"Hi [Name], just wanted to see if you had any questions or thoughts about the proposal. Happy to clarify anything or tweak the package if you need."

Or:

"I know you wanted some time to think—no rush at all. Just so you know, I do have a couple onboarding spots open next week if you'd like to move forward." This reminds them you're around and available but there's no pressure.

If they're still on the fence, offer a low-risk way to start:

- A one-time clean-up or audit
- A discounted first month
- A short-term trial
- A "starter package" with a limited scope

This lowers the barrier for them and lets them see your value up close.

Sometimes, a little reframe helps, too:

"I totally get wanting to think it over. Just remember—the longer your books stay messy, the harder it gets to catch up. Even a small step now saves you time and stress later."

That's a bit of urgency, but still low-key.

Bottom line: "I need to think about it" isn't a blow-off. It's just a request for more reassurance. Give them clarity, show some empathy and lay out the options. When people feel supported, saying yes gets a lot easier.

How to Handle Objections About Your Lack of Experience

When you're just starting out as a bookkeeper, you'll probably hear this a lot: "*I want someone with more experience*". It's a fair thing to ask, especially when people are trusting you with their money. However, here's the truth—being new doesn't mean you're not good at what you do. You just need to show them what you bring to the table right now.

Shift the Focus to What You Offer

Clients care about results, not just your job history. Don't apologise for being new. Instead, talk about what you've done to get ready:

"I'm early in my bookkeeping career but I've put a lot into training, systems and client care. I'm organised, I respond quickly and I always deliver clean, accurate books, every single time."

This way, you're showing them your reliability rather than your résumé.

Highlight Your Strengths

You might not have a long track record but you do have:

- A clear process for getting new clients started
- Experience with popular bookkeeping software like QuickBooks, Xero or Wave
- Templates and checklists to keep things consistent
- A strong work ethic and serious attention to detail
- A real passion for helping small businesses succeed

Be upfront about these. They help build trust.

Make It Easy for Them to Start

To help clients feel comfortable, offer something low-risk:

- A one-time clean-up or audit
- A discounted first month
- A short trial period
- A satisfaction guarantee or a "pause anytime" policy

This gives people a chance to see how you work—without any pressure.

Share Social Proof, Even If It's Casual

No official testimonials yet? No problem. Share:

- Feedback from mentors, peers or even practice clients
- Positive comments from Upwork, Fiverr or other freelance sites
- Any background you have in admin, finance or business support
- Relevant certifications or training

Even a simple quote like, "You're so organized—I'd trust you with my books any time", can make a difference.

Show Why Being New Can Be Good

Sometimes your fresh start is a selling point:

"I'm building my client list so I can offer more personal attention and flexible pricing than big firms. You're not just another account. You're a priority."

That makes your lack of experience feel like an advantage, not a drawback.

The Bottom Line: Yes, experience matters, but so does attitude, preparation and professionalism. When you lead with honesty, empathy and a clear offer, clients will look past your résumé and trust you with their books.

Payment Terms and Getting Deposit Commitments

Setting up clear payment terms isn't just a box to tick—it's how you protect your time, keep your cash flow healthy and show clients you mean business. Whether you're selling monthly packages or one-off cleanups, clients need to know what you expect and when. To be honest, a deposit does more than cover your bases financially. It shows commitment from both sides.

Here's how you can lay out your payment terms and lock in those deposits:

Why Payment Terms Matter

When you make your payment terms clear, you avoid awkward conversations and late payments. It lets people know you're reliable and serious about your work. It helps you plan your income and workload; you also dodge the mess of unpaid tasks or endless scope creep. Clients will feel better too—they'll know exactly what they're paying for and when.

What to Put in Your Payment Terms

Spell things out in your proposal or engagement letter. Make it easy to find and understand. Cover these basics:

– How often you'll bill (monthly, per project, or after key milestones).

– When payments are due (like, "Invoices go out on the 1st, due in seven days")

– Which payment methods you accept (bank transfer, PayPal, Stripe, whatever works).

– What happens if they pay late (this is optional but it helps set boundaries).

– How much deposit you need, especially for new clients or big jobs.

– Cancellation terms ("Need 14 days' notice to pause or stop services").

Don't overcomplicate it. Keep it simple and to the point.

Getting Deposit Commitments

Deposits are pretty standard, especially with new clients. They show the client is serious and you're not stuck doing free prep work.

You can say something like:

"To book your onboarding and get started, I ask for a 50% deposit. This way we're both committed and I can reserve your spot."

Or:

"For new clients, I take a one-time deposit before kicking things off. It's just part of my process to make sure everything goes smoothly for both of us."

Adjust the amount if you need—25–50% is common for projects. If you're doing monthly retainers, ask for the first month up front.

How to Make Payment Collection Easier

Use invoicing tools such as QuickBooks, Xero or Wave to automate things. Send invoices promptly and make sure your descriptions are clear. Add payment links or instructions right in the email. If someone's late, follow up politely. Always send receipts or confirmations so clients know their payment went through.

If you're working on a freelance platform like Upwork, deposits usually go through escrow automatically. Use that to your advantage.

Bottom line: Clear payment terms and upfront deposits save you headaches, build trust and set the stage for a professional relationship. When you're upfront about your process, clients respect it—and they'll pay on time.

When to Walk Away from "Bad-Fit" Clients

Not every prospect is a good match and that's perfectly fine. If you say yes to someone who doesn't fit, you end up drained, your workflow gets messy and your reputation can take a hit. The best bookkeepers know when to walk away — and they do it confidently. Protect your time, your values and your business.

How to Spot a Bad-Fit Client

Keep an eye out for these warning signs:

- They're rude, abrupt or just plain disrespectful when they talk to you.

- They expect complicated work for a bargain price.

- The project keeps growing but the pay doesn't.

- They're disorganised — missing documents, unclear processes, messy records.

- Payments show up late or they push back on deposits.

- They don't trust you or try to micromanage everything.

- Your values or working styles don't line up.

If you constantly feel anxious, undervalued or tense after talking to them, that's a sign.

Trust Your Gut

You don't need a spreadsheet of reasons. If something feels off, it probably is. Your gut is a business tool; don't ignore it.

"If you dread seeing their email on Monday morning, they're not your ideal client."

How to Walk Away Without Burning Bridges

Once you know it's not a match, be clear and respectful. You can say:

"Thanks for considering me. Based on what you've shared, I'm not the best fit for your needs right now. Wishing you all the best with your business."

Or:

"After looking at the scope and expectations, I think someone with a different approach would serve you better. I appreciate you reaching out."

You don't have to over-explain or apologise. You're just looking out for your business.

Why Saying No Matters

- You have more time for clients who actually fit.

- You protect your energy and reputation.

- You reinforce your boundaries.

- You build a business you actually enjoy running.

Saying no is a skill — and it shows growth.

The Bottom Line: Walking away from a bad-fit client isn't failure. It's leadership. When you stick to your boundaries and trust your instincts, you end up with a business that works for you.

Chapter 9: Onboarding Your First Clients

The Client Onboarding Checklist

Getting onboarding right can make all the difference. When you start off organised and prepared, clients notice. They see you as someone who's not only professional but also genuinely ready to get to work.

No matter if you're teaming up with a solopreneur or a small business on the rise, this checklist keeps things on track. It helps you grab the info you need, sort out expectations and dodge annoying problems down the road.

Here's a straightforward onboarding checklist you can use with every new client:

Before You Dive In

- Don't get started until you've:

- Sent out your engagement letter or service agreement — and got it back, signed

- Agreed on payment terms and collected any required deposit

- Set up a kick-off call or onboarding meeting

- Created a secure spot to share files (Google Drive, Dropbox, a client portal—whatever you prefer)

What to Ask Your Client For

Right from the start, request these:

- Business name, structure, and contact info

- Access to their bookkeeping software (QuickBooks, Xero, Wave, etc.)

- Recent bank and credit card statements (last 3–6 months)
- Login details or at least view-only access to bank feeds
- Past financial reports or tax filings, if they have them handy
- Info on their invoicing and payment systems (PayPal, Stripe, Square etc.)
- Any bills, invoices or receipts that are still hanging out there
- Their chart of accounts—or ask if you should set one up

Pro tip: Use your own branded intake form or checklist to collect all this smoothly. Makes you look sharp and saves everyone time.

Set Expectations and Nail Down the Workflow

During your first call or email back-and-forth, make sure you clear up:

- Exactly what services and deliverables you're providing
- How often they'll get reports and check-ins from you
- Best way to keep in touch (email, phone, portal—pick what works)
- Monthly deadlines for tasks like reconciliation and reporting
- Who's in charge of uploading or sending over documents
- Any special requirements for their industry or season (sales tax, 1099s etc.)

Sort all this out early, and you'll avoid confusion later. Plus, it shows you've got things handled right from the start.

Get Your Systems Up and Running

Once you have access, dive in and get things set up:

- Hook up the bank feeds and pull in all the past data.
- Take a good look at the chart of accounts and tidy things up.
- Add recurring tasks or reminders to your workflow so nothing slips through the cracks.
- Set up a client folder with clear names so it's easy to find what you need later.
- Do a first-month review to spot any weird entries or missing info.

First Report and Feedback

After you finish the first round:

- Send over the first financial report, along with a short summary.
- Ask for feedback and encourage questions.
- Tweak your process to fit what your client prefers.
- Lock in the ongoing schedule and outline the next steps.

All of this shows you're on top of things and helps build trust right from the start.

Bottom line: When you use a clear onboarding checklist, you look organised, prepared and reliable. It keeps things less stressful for everyone and lays the groundwork for a strong, smooth partnership.

Getting Financial Documents and Access

Once your client signs on, it's time to get your hands on the documents and system access you'll need. This part matters—it's what keeps your bookkeeping accurate, your workflow smooth and your reports on time. Nail this step, and your client will trust you right out of the gate.

Now, how do you actually get what you need without drowning your client in requests? Here's a simple way to do it:

What to Ask Your Client For

Send over a straightforward checklist. Spell out exactly what you need:

System Access:

- Bookkeeping software logins (like QuickBooks, Xero, or Wave)
- View-only or accountant access to bank and credit card accounts
- Access to payment platforms (PayPal, Stripe, Square)
- Access to invoicing or POS systems (HoneyBook, Shopify, SquareSpace)
- Payroll provider access, if they use one

Most clients have no idea how to give secure access so include clear instructions or links that walk them through it.

Financial Documents

- The last 3–6 months of bank and credit card statements
- Any outstanding invoices and bills
- Last year's tax return (if they have it)
- A chart of accounts—or permission to make one for them
- Loan or financing documents
- Receipts or expense records, especially for cash purchases

If they're coming from another bookkeeper, ask for a handover file or an export of their records.

Make It Easy For Everyone

- Use tools that make sharing safe and simple:
- Google Drive or Dropbox for shared folders
- Client portals if your CRM or practice management software has one
- Password managers like LastPass or 1Password for sharing credentials
- Intake forms to collect business info and preferences in one place

The easier you make this, the faster you'll be ready to get started.

How to Ask Without Overwhelming

Keep your request simple and friendly. Try something like: "To kick things off, I'll just need a few documents and access points from you. I've attached a checklist to make it easier. You can upload everything to our shared folder or just email them to me directly. If you have any questions or get stuck anywhere, let me know—I'm happy to help."

Let them know you'll keep everything safe and secure. Remind them they don't have to get it perfect—just send what they can.

Follow Up and Confirm

When the documents start coming in, reply quickly. Thank them, confirm you've received everything and point out if anything's missing. Tell them what happens next—when you'll review things or send your first update. Then, get rolling with your onboarding process.

This builds trust right away. They'll see you're organised and on top of things.

Key Takeaway: Collecting financial documents doesn't have to be a headache. With a straightforward checklist, secure sharing and a calm approach, you make it easy for your clients—and start things off on a good note.

Setting Expectations and Communication Rhythms

Building solid client relationships really comes down to two things: being clear about what you'll deliver and keeping the lines of communication open. When clients know exactly what's happening—and when—it puts everyone at ease. No surprises, no confusion. That's how you avoid scope creep, cut down on misunderstandings and earn trust that actually lasts.

How do you set the right tone from the start?

What to Nail Down Early

Right from that first call or during onboarding, spell these things out:

- What's included in your services, and what's off the table
- How long it takes to get reports, reconciliations, answers to questions—lay it all out
- When you need documents or approvals from them
- What the client's responsible for, like uploading receipts or sending over invoices
- How payments work—when you'll bill, what you need as a deposit, and what happens if someone's late
- How often you'll review things together—monthly, quarterly, or whatever fits

Get all this in writing. Drop it into your engagement letter, welcome packet or even a simple onboarding email.

Setting Up Communication Rhythms

No one likes chasing people down. You don't want to and your client definitely doesn't either. Set up a schedule that works for both of you. Tell clients how you'll stay in touch, when you'll check in and the best way for them to reach you. That way, everyone stays in the loop—no guesswork, just smooth sailing.

Example:

Rhythm Type	Example Frequency	Purpose
Monthly Check-In	1st or 15th of each month	Review reports, flag issues
Weekly Reminder	Every Monday or Friday	Request missing docs or updates
Quarterly Review	End of each quarter	Discuss trends, goals, adjustments
Ad-Hoc Alerts	As needed	Notify of urgent issues or changes

How I Like to Communicate

"Here's what works for me:

- I use email for official stuff—updates, reports, anything that needs a record.
- If we're onboarding or doing a review, let's reach for the phone or Zoom. It's just easier to talk things out.
- For quick questions, messaging apps are fine, if we both use them.
- I try to respond to emails within 24–48 hours, Monday to Friday. Keeps things manageable and stops burnout before it starts."

Let's Check In Regularly

As your business grows, things change. Every few months, let's pause and look at what's working:

- What's in (or out of) scope
- How you want reports
- How often we talk
- The pricing and packages

A short quarterly review keeps us on the same page and shows I'm paying attention.

Bottom line: Setting clear expectations isn't just paperwork—it's real leadership. When clients know the drill and how to reach you, they trust you more, lean on you less and stick around longer.

How to Build Systems That Scale Past 10 Clients

Handling a few clients feels pretty manageable but once your list grows past ten, things change rapidly. Suddenly, your old ways just can't keep up. If you don't set up smarter systems, you'll hit a wall — burnout, missed deadlines and uneven service aren't far behind. The trick is to lock in processes you can repeat every time so you stay organized, efficient and ready for whatever comes your way, no matter how many clients you take on.

Want to future-proof your bookkeeping business? Here's what actually works:

Set Up a Workflow You Can Use Every Time

Don't reinvent the wheel for each client. Build a checklist you follow for everyone, start to finish:

- Onboarding — intake form, set up access, send a welcome email.
- Monthly tasks — reconciliation, reporting, check in with the client.
- Quarterly review — look for trends, make adjustments, share recommendations.
- Offboarding — deliver final reports, remove access, ask for feedback.

Templates and automation are your friends here. The less you have to do by hand, the better.

Get Your Digital Space in Order

Your files need to make sense or you'll waste hours digging for stuff:

- Give each client his own folder, with subfolders for every month or quarter.
- Stick to a clear naming system (like "2025-10 Bank Reconciliation").
- Set up shared folders so clients can upload documents easily (Google Drive, Dropbox, whatever you use).
- Archive old clients so your workspace stays clean.

Do this and you'll always know where things are — even if you haven't touchec a file in months.

Pick Tools That Can Grow With You

Don't get stuck with software that holds you back. Grab tools that can keep ur as your business expands:

Tool Type	Recommended Features
Bookkeeping software	Multi-client dashboard, automation, integrations
Project mamagement	Task tracking, recurring reminders, client timelines
CRM or client portal	Contact info, notes, document sharing, onboarding forms
Time tracking and billing	Invoice generation, payment tracking, reporting

Think QuickBooks, Xero HQ, ClickUp, Trello, Dubsado or Practice Ignition They're popular for a reason—they work and they scale.

Automate Your Communication

Templates and scheduling tools save you from writing the same emails over anc over. Use them for monthly check-ins, delivering reports, payment reminders follow-ups and all those onboarding or offboarding messages. Clients stay ir the loop, and you get your time back.

Delegate and Outsource

You can't do everything. As more clients roll in, bring on a virtual assistant to handle admin work. Find a junior bookkeeper for routine data entry. Outsource payroll or tax prep if those aren't your thing. When things get busy, hire contractors for those seasonal rushes. Even just five hours of help a month makes a noticeable difference.

Keep an Eye on Your Numbers

Don't let your business run on autopilot. Set up a simple dashboard to track how many clients you have, how many hours you spend on each, what you're earning per client and your overall profit margins. If something looks off—maybe you're overloaded or not charging enough—you'll spot it quickly and can tweak things before you burn out.

Bottom line: Getting past 10 clients isn't about putting in more hours. It's about getting smarter with your systems, your tools and your boundaries. When you do that, your business grows, your clients stay happy and you actually get to enjoy the ride.

Chapter 10: Doing the Work Confidently

Monthly Bookkeeping Workflow Template

If you want reliable bookkeeping, you need a steady monthly routine. It's how you keep records tidy, catch mistakes before they turn into problems and juggle a bunch of clients without losing your mind. It doesn't matter if you handle one account or twenty; this template gives you a clear path to follow so you can stay organised and actually enjoy the process.

Here's a practical monthly workflow you can tweak or automate as your business picks up speed:

Week 1: Collect Documents & Check Bank Feeds

- Reach out to your client and remind him to upload his receipts, invoices and bills.

- Go over bank feeds and payment platforms to spot any missing or disconnected accounts.

- Take a quick look at last month's notes for anything still hanging or needing follow-up.

- Flag anything odd in the transactions and ask the client for details.

Pro tip: A shared folder or client portal makes uploading way easier for everyone.

Week 2: Categorize Transactions & Reconcile Accounts

- Sort all transactions in your bookkeeping software.

- Reconcile bank and credit card accounts with the statements.

- Match income and expenses to invoices and bills.

- Clean up any duplicate or uncategorized entries.

- Jot down anything you need the client to explain.

- Use tags or notes to keep track of questions or items still open.

Week 3: Reporting & Review

- Run the Profit & Loss and Balance Sheet reports.

- Check the numbers for accuracy, spot any trends or catch weird outliers.

- Write a short summary in plain language for your client.

- Send the reports along with a quick email or a link to his dashboard.

- Ask for feedback or questions.

- If your client likes visuals, toss in some charts or comparisons to help clarify things.

Week 4: Follow-Up & Look Ahead

- Circle back on anything still unresolved.

- Make sure your client received the reports and understands them.

- Note any changes in his business or new plans on the horizon.

- Update your task tracker or CRM to close out the month.

- Get ready for next month: set up recurring invoices, mark payroll dates, whatever's coming up.

- Use this week to build a better relationship and look for ways you can add more value.

Optional Add-Ons (For Clients Who Need More)

- Sales tax tracking and filing
- 1099 or VAT prep
- Inventory or job costing updates
- Budget vs. actual comparisons
- Custom KPI dashboards

You can offer these extras as premium services or bundle them into upgraded packages.

Bottom line: When you stick to a solid monthly workflow, your service stays consistent, your clients always know what's going on, and your business can actually grow without chaos. With clear steps and a few smart tools, you'll be able to deliver top-notch bookkeeping every month.

Common Mistakes New Bookkeepers Make (and How to Avoid Them)

Every new bookkeeper trips up now and then. It's just part of getting started. Still, a lot of headaches can be avoided if you set up the right systems and boundaries from the get-go. Spot these classic mistakes early and you'll run a business that's accurate, sustainable and keeps your clients happy.

Let's dig into the most common missteps—and how you can dodge them:

1. Not Setting Clear Boundaries

Here's the trap: You say yes to everything. You work outside your scope. You answer client messages at 10 p.m. It's exhausting.

How do you fix this?

Spell out - on paper - exactly what you offer. Set clear hours and stick to them. Use a welcome packet or onboarding guide so clients know what to expect. Don't be afraid to say, "That's not included—need me to quote for that?"

Boundaries aren't just about protecting your schedule—they keep you sane.

2. Messy Document Management

You lose files. You mix up folders. You're not sure which version is the latest. Suddenly, you're drowning in chaos.

How do you get organized?

Create the same folder structure for every client. Name your files clearly (think "2025-10 P&L – ClientName"). Store it all in a secure, cloud-based system. Keep a checklist of what you need each month.

Good organisation isn't just nice—it's your secret weapon.

3. Avoiding Client Communication

You get busy or stuck on something; next thing you know, you go quiet. Maybe you're not sure how to explain an issue so you put it off.

How do you stay connected?

Set regular check-ins—monthly or quarterly is fine. Use templates to send reports or updates. If you're running behind or need more info, just say so. Clients care more about honest updates than perfect answers. Open communication builds trust that lasts.

4. Doing Everything Manually

You're typing in transactions by hand, chasing receipts, building every report from scratch. It eats up your time and energy.

How do you work smarter?

Lean on automation: bank feeds, recurring invoices, rules. Build templates for reports, emails and onboarding. Invest in software that will grow with you. Track your time to spot where you're spinning your wheels. Automation frees you up for the work that matters.

5. Undercharging or Undervaluing Your Work

You start out cheap—maybe out of fear or just not knowing what to charge. Later, you regret it.

How do you fix your pricing?

Check what others charge and price based on the *value* you deliver, not just your hours. Offer different packages so clients can choose what fits. Review your rates at least once a year. Remember: You're not just "doing books". You're giving clients peace of mind. Charge for it.

6. Ignoring Your Own Business Finances

You spend all your energy on client books, but *your own* accounts fall by the wayside.

How do you turn that around?

Block out time every month to reconcile your own books. Track your income expenses and hours by client. Set and review your business goals every quarter. *Treat your business as your best client*—because if you don't measure, you can't grow.

Key Takeaway: Mistakes are going to happen but they don't have to run the show. When you set up clear systems, hold your boundaries and keep learning you'll build a bookkeeping business that's not only profitable but one you'll actually enjoy running.

When to Ask for Help or Bring in a Mentor

Building a bookkeeping business feels great but let's be real—it isn't always smooth sailing. Sometimes you'll hit a wall. Maybe you're overwhelmed second-guessing everything or just plain stuck. That's not failing. That's just your cue to reach out.

Getting help—or working with a mentor—can speed up your progress sharpen your skills and save you months or even years of spinning your wheels.

When should you actually ask for help? Here's what to watch for:

You don't have to wait until you're underwater. Reach out if you notice yourself:

- Spending way too much time searching for answers or doubting your choices
- Unsure how to set your prices, package your services or stand out
- Struggling with client boundaries, scope creep or chasing late payments
- Feeling isolated or stuck comparing yourself to others
- Wanting to grow but having no clue how to scale without burning out
- Making mistakes you know you could avoid with the right advice

If you keep wondering, "Am I even doing this right?" more than once a week, it's probably time.

What a Mentor or Coach Really Does

A good mentor isn't just someone who doles out advice. He can give you real perspective, hold you accountable and show you shortcuts you wouldn't find on your own. Depending on what you need, a mentor can help you:

- Fine-tune your services and pricing
- Upgrade your onboarding and how you talk to clients
- Build systems that actually scale
- Handle tricky client situations without losing your cool
- Create a business that fits your life, not the other way around

Maybe you just need one session or maybe you want ongoing support. Either way, the right mentor will help you move faster—and with a whole lot more confidence.

Where to Find the Support You Need

You don't have to figure it all out alone. Here's where to look:

- Industry Facebook groups or LinkedIn communities
- Bookkeeping forums and online memberships
- Local business networks or co-working spaces
- Freelance platforms that offer coaching
- Paid mentorship programs or business coaches
- Peer accountability groups or masterminds

Start by asking yourself, "Who's already doing what I want to do—and how can I learn from them?" That's usually the best place to begin.

How to Ask for Help (Without Feeling Awkward)

Try something like this when you reach out:

"Hello [Name], I've been following your work and really admire what you do. I'm starting my own bookkeeping business and have a few questions. If you offer mentorship, I'd love to learn more. Either way, thanks for your time!"

Most people with experience are pretty open to helping out, especially if you're upfront and respectful.

Key Takeaway: There's nothing weak about asking for help. Actually, it's the smartest move you can make. The quicker you reach out, the quicker you'll get your business running the way you want. Good mentors help you see through the fog. Suddenly, you're not just grinding alone — you're growing with purpose.

Quality Assurance Before Delivering Reports

Clean, accurate reports do more than just check off requirements; they build trust. Clients count on you for a clear picture of their finances and even a small mistake can shake their trust. That's why sticking to a solid quality assurance process isn't optional; it's a must before you send out any reports, whether it's monthly or quarterly.

Here's how to check your work like a pro — and hit send with confidence every single time:

Your Pre-Delivery QA Checklist

Before you send anything out, take a minute to run through this:

1. Reconciliation Review

Make sure all your bank and credit card accounts are fully reconciled. Double-check for any unreconciled transactions or duplicates—those tend to sneak in. Your statement balances should match your software, right down to the last cent.

2. Transaction Accuracy

Look over how you've categorised everything—does it all make sense? Flag anything that seems off or hasn't been categorized yet. Also make sure that income and expenses line up with how your client actually does business.

3. Report Consistency

Pull up the Profit & Loss, Balance Sheet and Cash Flow reports (if you need that last one). Watch for any negative balances or weird spikes. Compare the numbers to previous months to catch anything unusual or spot trends. Double-check that the dates on the reports match the period you're reporting on.

4. Client-Specific Checks

If your client uses custom categories or tags, make sure they're correct. Include sales tax, payroll or inventory details if those matter for this client. Take a second look at any manual journal entries or adjustments—little mistakes can hide there.

5. Presentation & Delivery

Add a quick summary or a few comments to highlight what matters most. Stick to consistent formatting and clear names for your files (like "2025-10 P&L – ClientName"). Save everything as a PDF or drop it in the secure client portal. Always include a friendly, professional message when you send the report.

Bonus Tip: Use a QA Template

Build a QA checklist you can reuse—either in your project management tool or as a printed form. It's easy to overlook things when you're busy or juggling lots of clients; having a template keeps you on track.

Invite Feedback

When you send the report, ask something like: "Let me know if anything looks off or if you want to talk through the numbers together". This lets your client know you're on his side and care about the details.

Key Takeaway: Quality assurance isn't just about catching mistakes—it's about giving your clients peace of mind. When you stick to a solid review process, you show your clients they can count on you to get it right. That's how you become the bookkeeper they trust.

Chapter 11: Turning Clients Into Referral Engines

When and How to Ask for Referrals

Happy clients are your secret weapon. However, most won't send folks your way unless you nudge them a little. Asking for referrals isn't begging—it's more like inviting people who already trust you to help others. Do it correctly and you'll end up with stronger relationships and a steady stream of new clients - all without feeling pushy.

How do you actually ask for referrals without making it weird? Here's how to turn great service into steady growth:

When to Ask for a Referral

Timing matters. Look for those moments when your client's happy—like right after they give you a compliment, when you've just finished a project that really helped them out or after you've wrapped up a successful onboarding. If they sound relieved or excited, that's your cue.

Right after a quarterly review or when you hit a big milestone works, too. Just watch for those signs of satisfaction; that's when they'll be most willing to share your name.

How to Ask (Without Making It Awkward)

Keep it casual and genuine. You might say something like, "I'm glad the reports are making things easier for you. If you know anyone else who needs help with his books, I'd love to help him out, too. Referrals really help me grow." Or "It's been awesome working with you. If you meet another business owner stressed about bookkeeping, feel free to send him my way—I'll take good care of him." You're just offering help, not making a sales pitch.

Make Referring You a Breeze

Don't make them jump through hoops. Add a quick referral blurb to your email signature. Set up a simple form or referral page on your site. Share a ready-to-send message or a branded PDF they can forward. Give them a few talking points about what you do best. The easier you make it, the more likely they'll actually refer you.

If You Want, Sweeten the Deal

If it fits your style, offer a little something as a thank-you—a discount on their next invoice, a free consultation, a handwritten note or maybe even a donation to a cause they care about. Make sure it feels like genuine appreciation, not a bribe.

Always Say Thanks

When someone sends you a referral, thank him personally. Let him know what happened, even if it doesn't turn into new business right away. Celebrate the effort. It shows you value the relationship. Next time, he'll be even more willing to refer you.

Bottom line: Referrals grow from trust, not tricks. Ask when the moment's right, make it easy and show real gratitude. When your clients feel appreciated they'll spread the word without you even having to ask twice.

How to Create a Simple Referral Incentive Program

Referrals can do wonders for your bookkeeping business. When happy clients talk you up, you get the kind of trust money can't buy. Still, even the most satisfied clients sometimes need a little push to actually tell their friends about you. That's where a **referral incentive program** comes in. You give people a reason to act and, at the same time, remind them why your service matters.

Here's a straightforward way to set up a referral program that gets results—without coming off as desperate or salesy:

Step 1: Set Your Goal

Figure out what you want your referral program to do. Are you looking for more of your dream clients? Want people talking about your services more often? Maybe you just want to thank your loyal clients for helping you grow. Set a clear goal. Keep it simple and manageable, especially if you're new to this.

Step 2: Pick Your Reward

Choose an incentive that feels like a real thank you but won't break the bank. It should be something your clients will actually care about. Options could be:

Incentive Type	Example
Cash reward	$50 for each successful referral
Invoice discount	10-20% off next month's service
Free service	One-time mini-audit or report review
Gift card	Amazon, coffee shop or local business
Charity donation	$25 donated in their name

Pick a reward that actually fits your brand and the people you serve. Some folks want real savings, others just appreciate a thoughtful "thank you".

Step 3: Set the Rules

Don't overcomplicate things. Make it clear:

- Who can refer (maybe current or past clients)
- What makes a referral count (like when someone signs a contract or pays their first invoice)
- How and when you'll hand out the reward
- Any limits (for example, up to three referrals a year)

Try something like this:

"Refer another business owner and get $50 off your next invoice when they sign up for monthly services. No limits—just gratitude."

Step 4: Get the Word Out (Without Pushing)

Let people know about your referral program but don't bombard them. Slip it into your welcome email. Add a quick note in your email signature. Mention it during your monthly check-ins or when you send out reports. Maybe design a simple referral card or PDF they can easily forward. Every now and then, post about it on LinkedIn or in your favorite business groups. Always keep it as a thank-you, not a sales pitch.

Step 5: Track and Celebrate

Keep track of every referral and reward. When someone sends you a new lead, thank him personally. Send the reward right away. Celebrate the moment, even if that referral doesn't turn into a client right away. It shows you care and makes people want to refer again.

Bottom line: A good referral incentive program turns happy clients into true partners in your growth. When it's easy, genuine and worth their while, referrals become second nature, not just a stroke of luck.

Getting Testimonials from Satisfied Clients

Testimonials work wonders. They show real proof, build trust and help new clients feel good about choosing you. Still, lots of bookkeepers hold back from asking or they wait until it's way too late. But here's the thing—happy clients are usually glad to help out, as long as you keep it easy and respectful.

How do you actually ask for testimonials without it feeling weird? Here's a simple breakdown:

Why Testimonials Matter

- They help new clients trust you.
- They show off your strengths—in your client's own words.
- They remind everyone of your value and professionalism.

- You can use them almost anywhere: your website, proposals, social media.

Even a quick line like, "Susan made my books make sense for the first time in years", can do a lot.

When to Ask for a Testimonial

Timing really matters. Ask right after you:

- Deliver a clean report or solve a tough problem.

- Hear the client thank you or share relief.

- Finish onboarding or a big clean-up.

- Wrap up a quarterly review or hit a big milestone.

Watch for those moments when your client's genuinely happy. That's your best shot.

How to Ask (Without Feeling Pushy)

Keep it friendly and straightforward:

"I'm glad you're happy with the service. Would you be willing to share a short testimonial for my website or proposals? Just a few lines about your experience would be amazing."

Or try:

"It's been great working with you. If you're comfortable, could I use a brief quote about your experience? No pressure!"

You're not begging for compliments. You're just inviting them to help others who need support.

Make It Easy to Respond

Don't make clients think too hard. Offer some prompts:

- What was your situation before we started?
- What changed after we worked together?
- What would you tell someone thinking about hiring me?

Give them a template or example. Let them reply however's easiest: email, form, text—whatever works. Offer to draft something based on their feedback for their approval. The simpler you make it, the more likely they'll actually respond.

Where to Use Testimonials

Once you've obtained them, don't let them sit in your inbox. Show them off:

- Put them on your website—right up front or on your services page.
- Add them to proposals and onboarding materials.
- Drop one in your email signature or referral messages.
- Share on LinkedIn or social media (get their okay first).
- Use them in printed materials or welcome kits.

Always check with your client before publishing—ask if they want their name, business or just initials shown.

Bottom line: Testimonials aren't just nice words—they're trust builders. Ask at the right time, make it easy and use them smartly to attract the clients you really want.

Building Case Studies with Everyday Results

You don't have to pull off huge turnarounds or save clients piles of money to create a case study that works. Sometimes the small stuff—fixing messy books, making things clearer or just saving someone a few hours—shows your value just as well. Case studies give people a real sense of what it's like to work with you and they help you build trust by sharing actual stories, not just promises.

Here's how to put together case studies that matter, even if the results aren't jaw-dropping:

Why Case Studies Work

- They tell a story, not just a list of numbers.

- They show off how you work and how you treat your clients.

- They help new clients see themselves in your old clients' shoes.

- They give you credibility, even if you're not a ten-year veteran.

Think of them as honest, down-to-earth success stories.

What to Include

Stick to four simple parts:

1. The Client: "A solo consultant with scattered books and no real financial reports." Don't worry about using the client's real name—initials or a description work fine.

2. The Problem: "They hadn't reconciled accounts in months and didn't really know what they earned each month." Lay out the issue clearly, even if it's basic.

3. What You Did: "I cleaned up three months of transactions, set up bank feeds and built a simple monthly report." Focus on how you tackled things, not just the end result.

4. The Outcome: "They get regular reports now, feel more confident about their numbers and save 4–6 hours every month." Don't downplay small wins—clarity, time and peace of mind matter.

Tips for Writing (Without Making It a Big Deal)

- Keep it short—150 to 300 words is plenty.

- Use plain English and skip the jargon.

- Talk about the client's experience, not just your side of things.

- Ask for a testimonial to go with your case study.

- Stick to a simple format so you can build a collection over time.

You can even turn a piece of client feedback into a mini case study—just add a quick intro and wrap-up.

Where to Share Your Case Studies

- Put them on your website—service or testimonial pages work great.

- Add them to proposals or onboarding packets.

- Drop them into referral messages or social media.

- Use them in a "client success" email series.

- Print them for welcome kits or other handouts.

They're flexible and they get more valuable as your business grows.

Bottom line: You don't need big wins to build trust. Even the basics—done well and shared clearly—can turn into case studies that attract the right clients

Scaling Your Business to 10 and Beyond

Chapter 12: The Progress Tracker

Tracking Your Outreach Activities

Once your bookkeeping business grows past ten clients, outreach stops being just friendly networking. It turns into a system—a real strategy. You're not just firing off a few emails or posting on LinkedIn here and there. You're reaching out, following up, going to events, sending DMs and juggling a bunch of leads.

If you don't track all this, things rapidly get messy. But when you do, you see patterns, you get organized - and you close more deals.

How do you turn outreach from a guessing game into a repeatable, data-driven machine?

It's not just cold emails. Outreach covers way more:

- Discovery calls and every follow-up
- Asking for referrals and sending thank-you notes
- Posts or comments on social media
- In-person events or online networking groups
- Email campaigns, newsletters, all that stuff
- Website enquiries and anyone filling out your lead forms
- Direct messages or intros on LinkedIn

Seriously, if it's a touchpoint that could land you a client, it counts. Track it.

Why Bother Tracking?

- You figure out what's actually working and what's just noise
- You don't lose leads just because you forgot to follow up

- You see how many times you need to reach out before someone signs up
- You can actually predict your growth and plan your workload
- You watch your progress build - and that gives you confidence

In the end, outreach is a numbers game. Tracking shows you the score.

What to Track (and How)

Use a simple spreadsheet, CRM or project management tool to log:

Field	Example Entry
Date	28 October 2025
Contact Name	John Smith
Business Name	JS Creatives
Channel	LinkedIn DM
Type of Outreach	Referral follow-up
Response Status	Replied, scheduled call
Next Step	Send proposal after call
Notes	Interested in monthly package

Check in every week and take a closer look each month—you'll start to notice patterns pop up.

Tag Everything

Don't just log your outreach. Tag it. Mark down where the lead came from. Was it a referral, social media, an event, your website? Note the industry: creative, retail, consulting, whatever fits. Track the stage, too. Is it still cold, warming up? Did you send a proposal, did you land the deal?

Don't forget the outcome: won, lost, paused or needs a follow-up. These tags make it way easier to see what's working so you can sharpen your message and zero in on the clients you really want.

Automate When You Can

As business picks up, bring in some tools. **Trello or ClickUp** can help you visualise your outreach. **Dubsado or HoneyBook** are solid for CRM and tracking leads. If you want something simple and flexible, **Google Sheets** works. **Zapier** will grab leads for you from forms or emails so you don't have to.

Start with the basics. As your client list grows, level up your system.

Bottom line: Outreach isn't just about putting in the hours; it's about being steady and clear. When you actually track what you're doing, all those random efforts turn into a real plan for growth. The more you keep tabs on things, the better you'll become.

Measuring Conversion Rates

What Is Conversion Rate?

Conversion rate shows you the percentage of people who go from "maybe" to "I'm in". It's a straightforward way to see if your outreach, your discovery calls or your proposals are actually working. If that number's going up, you know you're on the right track.

When you start reaching out to more people, you need to know what's landing and what's falling flat. Conversion rate is a big deal here. It shows you, plainly and simply, how many leads end up turning into real, paying clients. If you keep an eye on this number, you can tweak your messaging, tighten up your follow-ups and actually grow your business without just guessing.

How do you measure conversion rates and, once you have that number, what do you do with it?

Here's the basic formula:

$$\text{Conversion Rate} = \left(\frac{\text{Number of Clients Who Said Yes}}{\text{Number of Leads or Inquiries}}\right) \times 100$$

For example, if you spoke to 20 leads and signed 4 clients, your conversion rate would be 20%.

Why Conversion Rate Matters

Conversion rate isn't just a number you track out of habit—it tells you whether or not your outreach and sales actually work. It points out where clients get stuck or drop off so you don't have to guess what's wrong.

When you watch this number, you get a much better grip on how much you're likely to grow and what your income looks like down the road. It also nudges you when it's time to shake up your messaging, rethink your pricing or switch up your packages. For instance, if you notice people slipping away after you close the deal, that's your cue to tighten up your follow-up or make onboarding smoother.

Conversion rate gives you real feedback, every step of the way.

What to Track

To measure conversion accurately, track:

Metric	Description
Leads generated	Total number of enquiries or prospects
Discovery calls held	Number of actual conversations
Proposals sent	Number of formal offers made
Clients signed	Number of paying clients onboarded
Conversion rate	Clients divided by leads X 100

You can also track conversion by source (e.g., referrals, social media, website or networking) to see which are the best-performing channels.

Once you have your numbers, here's how to actually use that data:

Pick out some monthly or quarterly targets. See how your conversion rates stack up between different outreach methods. If you notice leads start fading away after your calls, tweak your follow-up routine.

If people freeze up during proposals or onboarding, that's a sign to smooth out those areas. When something's working, celebrate it and do more of it. Even tiny bumps in your conversion rate can make a real difference for your bottom line.

Here's the takeaway: Conversion rate isn't just some sales stat—it's your roadmap for growth. Track it regularly and you'll make sharper decisions, give clients a better experience and grow your business with a lot more confidence.

Adjusting Your Approach Based on What's Working

Growing your bookkeeping business isn't just about taking on more work. It's about focusing on what's actually bringing results. As you keep an eye on your outreach, conversion rates, client feedback and how you deliver your services, you'll start to see patterns.

Some strategies just work better. Some offers connect more. Some clients are simply easier—and more profitable—to serve. The trick is to spot what's working and lean in.

Here's how to sharpen your approach and stay flexible:

Review Your Metrics Regularly

Block out time each month or quarter to dig into the numbers:

- Where are your best clients coming from? Which channels are pulling their weight?
- Which outreach methods land the most new clients?
- What do clients rave about—and what trips them up?
- Which services eat up more time than they should?
- Which packages actually pay off for the time you put in?

Don't just go with your gut. Let the data steer you.

Keep What Works, Fix What Doesn't

Once you spot a winning pattern:

- Double up on what's working—use the same messaging, platforms or timing that brought results.

- Fine-tune your offers—change up pricing, package details or scope if you see better uptake.

- Streamline your workflow—automate or create templates for anything that slows you down.

- Cut the dead weight—stop offering services or using channels that just aren't worth it.

Scaling up is about focusing, not just adding more.

Listen to Your Clients

Your clients will tell you what matters if you listen. Pay attention when someone says:

- "That report really helped."
- "I wish things were clearer here..."
- "I didn't know you offered that."
- "This part was confusing or took too long."

Use their feedback to tighten up your onboarding, communication and service experience. Even small changes can make clients stick around longer.

Stay Nimble with Your Messaging

If certain words, offers or visuals pull in more attention, keep using them. If something flops, change it up. Test everything:

- Subject lines and email intros
- Social media captions and hashtags

- Website headlines and service descriptions
- Proposal formats and follow-up routines

Marketing never really ends—it's all about testing and tweaking.

Document What's Working

Build yourself a "What's Working" playbook:

- Templates that get the best response
- Onboarding steps that work every time
- Service packages that make you the most money
- Client types or industries that respond fastest

This becomes your cheat sheet for growth—and makes it way easier to train new team members down the road.

Bottom line: Scaling isn't about doing it all. It's about doing the right things and doing them better. Track what's working, adjust along the way and you'll build a business that's not just bigger but smarter and more profitable.

Staying Motivated Through Rejection

Rejection is just part of the ride, not some statement about your value. You send out a bunch of emails, nobody replies. You get on a call, the client disappears. Maybe they just pick someone else. Yeah, it stings. Yet, every "no" gets you closer to a real "yes". The trick is to keep moving, even when it feels as if you're getting nowhere.

Here's how to stay motivated and keep your head in the game—even when everything feels slow:

See Rejection as a Detour, Not a Dead End

Not every lead should turn into a client. Sometimes, rejection actually saves you from taking on projects that'll just drain you or from working with people who aren't a fit.

Instead of thinking, "What did I mess up?" try asking:

- What can I take away from this?

- Was this even the right client for me?

- How can I make my process better next time?

That way, rejection actually makes you sharper.

Track What You Do, Not Just What You Get

If you only count wins by the number of clients you sign, you're missing the point.

Look at the actions:

- How many people did you reach out to?

- How many calls did you book?

- How many proposals did you send?

- Did you collect any testimonials?

- Are your systems better than last month?

- Do you feel more confident?

Every step counts. Even if you don't see results right away, you're still building momentum.

Get Used to Hearing "No"

Even the best in the business hear "no" a lot of the time. It's not about you—it's just timing, budgets, priorities or fit. Keep a little "rejection file" with positive feedback or kind words you've received so you can look back when you need a boost.

"Thanks for your time—I'm going with someone else, but I really appreciated your professionalism" - that counts as a win, too.

Protect Your Energy

Rejection hits harder when you're exhausted or working alone. Give yourself some space:

- Take breaks after outreach sprints.

- Talk to other people in your field.

- Celebrate tiny wins—even sending an email is progress.

- Keep a vision board or something that reminds you why you're doing this.

Your mindset is part of your business. Take care of it.

Just Keep Going

Honestly, the only way to actually fail is to quit. The more you put yourself out there, the more you learn and grow. Rejection isn't the end—it's just information. Every "no" helps you get closer to the right "yes."

Bottom line: Rejection isn't a roadblock. It's part of how you get where you're going. When you change how you look at it, track your progress and look after your mindset, you stay resilient and ready for whatever comes next.

Chapter 13: Common Pitfalls and How to Avoid Them

Underpricing Yourself Into Exhaustion

Many new bookkeepers fall into the trap of charging too little. Maybe it's fear. Maybe it's just wanting to land that first client or thinking you have to be "affordable" to get any work at all.

Honestly, underpricing does more than just shrink your paycheck. It drains your energy, breeds resentment and turns your business into a daily grind instead of something you actually enjoy. If you're hustling non-stop and still barely scraping by, it's time to take a hard look at what you're charging.

How do you know when you're underpricing? Well, here's what usually causes it:

- You're scared clients will walk away if you ask for more.

- You're comparing your rates to cheap DIY software or cut-rate competitors.

- You don't fully believe in the value you bring.

- You want to "help" your clients, even if it means shortchanging yourself.

- You forget to include admin time, taxes or other business costs in your prices.

It usually comes from a good place, but it just isn't sustainable.

What are the signs you're undercharging?

- You're working endless hours and still struggling to pay the bills.

- You get a knot in your stomach when clients pile on extra requests.

- You know you should raise your rates, but you're scared to do it—even as you get better at what you do.

- You end up with clients who don't respect your time.

- You say "yes" to everything, just to keep busy.

If you're exhausted and barely getting by, that's not ambition—it's a trap.

Here's how to break out of it and price yourself sustainably:

- Figure out your numbers—work out your minimum rate based on what you need for your time, expenses and goals.

- Price for value, not just hours. You're giving clients peace of mind and clarity, not just filling out spreadsheets.

- Offer packages at different levels so clients have options and you're not selling all your time for pennies.

- Review your rates regularly. Every 6 to 12 months, check in and raise them as your skills and demand grow.

- Own your prices. Explain them clearly and confidently.

You're not just punching numbers into a screen. You help clients find direction and stability in their business. That's worth more than you think.

How to Raise Rates Without Fear

Start with new clients first. Try out your new prices before you change things for everyone else. For your current clients, give them a heads up—30 to 60 days is fair and shows you respect their time.

When you explain the change, focus on the value you bring. Say something like, "As my services have grown, I'm updating my pricing to match the level of support I offer."

If some are worried, don't just leave them hanging. Offer a smaller package or let them adjust gradually with a phased increase. Some people will leave and that's okay. The right clients will stick around.

Raising your rates isn't the risky move—staying underpaid is what drains you. Here's what really matters: Underpricing your work just burns you out. Charge what you're worth. You'll draw better clients, protect your energy and finally build a business that gives back instead of taking everything you have.

Taking On Nightmare Clients Out of Desperation

When you're just starting out, or facing a slow month, it's tempting to say "yes" to any client who shows interest. However, desperation can lead to you making poor decisions.

Taking on nightmare clients may fill the gap short-term but they often cost you more in stress, time and reputation than they're worth. The truth is: not every client is a good fit; learning to say "no" is a sign of growth, not arrogance.

Here's how to spot red flags early and protect your business from burnout:

What Is a Nightmare Client?

They're not just demanding, they're draining. Common traits include:

- Constant scope creep without added pay
- Disrespectful or dismissive communication
- Chronic lateness with documents or payments
- Micro-managing or second-guessing your expertise
- Blaming you for their own disorganisation
- Ignoring boundaries or expecting 24/7 availability

Even one or two of these behaviours can derail your workflow and confidence.

Why We Say "Yes" Anyway:

- Fear of losing income
- Pressure to "build the portfolio"
- Belief that any client is better than none

- Hope that things will improve over time
- Lack of clarity around ideal client traits

Regrettably, desperation leads to depletion, not growth.

How to Avoid the Trap

- Define your ideal client profile — industry, attitude, responsiveness, budget
- Create a vetting process — discovery calls, intake forms, trial periods
- Set boundaries early — scope, communication hours, payment terms
- Trust your gut — if something feels off, it probably is
- Have a referral list — send misaligned leads to other professionals

Saying "no" to the wrong client creates space for the right one.

What to Say Instead of "Yes"

Here's a respectful way to decline:

"Thanks so much for reaching out. Based on your needs, I may not be the best fit at this time — but I'd be happy to refer you to someone who might be."

This protects your energy and your reputation.

Rebuild Without Regret

If you've already taken on a nightmare client:

- Set firmer boundaries immediately
- Revisit your contract and scope

- Plan a respectful offboarding if needed
- Reflect on what led to the decision — and how to prevent it next time

Every experience is a lesson, not a failure.

Key Takeaway: Desperation leads to depletion. When you choose clients intentionally — not reactively — you build a business that energises you, respects your time and grows sustainably.

Scope Creep and Boundary Issues

Scope creep sneaks up on you quickly, especially if you're running your bookkeeping business solo. It usually starts with a quick favour: a "can you just..." or "do you mind adding this?" and suddenly you're working extra hours you never billed for, expectations get fuzzy and the whole relationship starts to feel "off".

When you don't set clear boundaries, clients sometimes don't realise they're asking too much. That leaves you exhausted and underpaid.

How can you catch scope creep early? How do you set boundaries that actually stick so you can protect your time, energy and sanity?

What Scope Creep Looks Like

You'll know it when you see it. Clients ask for things you never agreed to. Little requests that pop up more and more, until they start feeling like regular tasks. Maybe you're getting unscheduled calls or urgent messages during your downtime. Maybe someone wants tax advice or payroll help but that's not even your area. Perhaps they pressure you to answer outside your working hours or skip steps just to be "faster". Most of the time it's not intentional but if you let it slide you'll pay the price.

Why Boundaries Get Blurry

Sometimes we worry about losing clients or letting them down so we say "yes" too often. Sometimes there's no written agreement spelling out what's included.

Maybe the onboarding process was vague. Perhaps you just want to help and go the extra mile—especially if you're new and not used to saying "no" in a professional way. Yet, boundaries aren't walls. They're just clear lines so everyone knows what to expect.

How to Prevent Scope Creep

Get specific about your scope. Spell out exactly what's included (and just as importantly, what's not) in your service agreement. Send a welcome packet that lays out when you're available, how quickly you'll respond, and what you expect from your client.

Track your time so you notice right away if you're doing more than you signed up for. Offer packages or add-ons so if someone wants something extra, there's a clear path—and a price—for that. Check in every few months and update your agreement if your client's needs change. The more you clarify up front, the less drama you'll have later.

How to Respond When Boundaries Get Crossed

It happens. Here's how you can handle it without burning bridges:

"I'd love to help with that! It's outside what we agreed on but I can quote it as an add-on if you'd like."

Or maybe:

"To keep things running smoothly, I stick to our workflow. If you need extra support, let's talk about some options."

You're not being difficult. You're just being professional.

Boundaries Help Everyone

When you set and stick to boundaries, your clients know what to expect from you. You deliver your best work, every time. You keep burnout and resentment at bay. Consequently, you build a business that values your time and expertise. Boundaries aren't just for you—they make the whole experience better for your clients, too.

Bottom line: Scope creep is sneaky but you don't have to let it take over. Clear communication, set packages and confident boundaries protect your business and help you serve your clients even better.

Imposter Syndrome Management

You know that nagging voice that says, "You're not really qualified", or "You just got lucky"? That's imposter syndrome. It shows up for a lot of bookkeepers, especially when you're new, changing careers or trying to grow your business. The funny thing is, feeling like an imposter usually just means you care about doing good work. The trick isn't to make those doubts disappear—it's learning how not to let them run the show.

How do you spot imposter syndrome? Here's what it looks like:

- You brush off your wins or downplay your skills.

- You feel like you're faking it, even when people tell you you're doing great.

- You keep comparing yourself to others with more experience.

- You steer clear of things like marketing or networking because you don't want the spotlight.

- You work yourself to the bone just to "prove" you belong.

It's not that you're not capable. It's just your mind playing tricks.

Let's talk about what actually helps:

1. Track Your Wins

Start a "confidence file". Save those glowing client emails, before-and-after shots of the books you've cleaned up, screenshots of positive feedback and notes about tough challenges you've handled. When doubt creeps in, look at that file. It's hard evidence that you're making a real difference.

2. Stick to the Facts

When your brain starts saying, "I'm not good enough", stop and ask yourself: Where's the proof? What have I actually done? Would I ever say this to a friend in my shoes? Push back against the story in your head with the real facts.

3. Find Your People

Join bookkeeping groups, mastermind circles or online forums. Pretty quickly you'll see that everyone has doubts. Everyone messes up sometimes. Everyone learns by doing. You're not alone and you're definitely not behind.

4. Celebrate Progress (Not Perfection)

You don't need to know everything to be valuable. Just keep showing up, keep learning and serve your clients with care. Confidence comes from doing, not waiting until you're "ready".

5. Keep Growing

Take a course, find a mentor or read up on the industry. Every new skill you build is another layer to your confidence.

When imposter thoughts show up, try these affirmations:

- I'm learning, growing and getting better every day.

- My work helps real people solve real problems.

- I don't have to be perfect to be valuable.

- I've earned my spot and I'm still moving forward.

Say them out loud. Jot them down. Come back to them any time.

Bottom line? Imposter syndrome is normal but it's not forever. With a little reflection, some community and steady action, you'll find your confidence and show up for your business in a whole new way.

Chapter 14: From 10 Clients to a Sustainable Practice

When to Stop Taking On New Clients

Watching your bookkeeping business grow feels great—until it starts spinning out of control. At some point, saying "yes" to every new client just makes things messy. Hitting the pause button isn't a failure. Honestly, it's a smart move. You're looking out for your clients, your sanity and the future of your business.

How do you know you've hit that limit? Here's what to watch for:

- You're working late, skipping breaks, or both, just to keep up.

- Reports, reconciliations or client follow-ups are piling up.

- Onboarding new clients feels rushed or chaotic.

- Every new enquiry brings a wave of anxiety or frustration.

- Clients start noticing delays or mistakes.

- You're ignoring your own business books or systems.

These aren't things to be proud of—they're warning signs.

Why Hitting Pause Makes Sense

Pressing pause gives you space to catch your breath and focus on what matters. You can deliver the service your current clients expect, tighten up your systems, rethink your pricing or bring in help if you need it. This is how you set yourself up for growth that lasts.

What to Say Instead of "Yes"

You don't have to leave people hanging. Try something like:

"Thank you for reaching out. Right now, I'm at full capacity so I can serve my current clients well. I'd be happy to add you to my waitlist or connect you with a trusted colleague."

Or you can:

- Start a waitlist and give people an idea of when you'll be available.

- Offer a discovery call, but with future openings in mind.

- Refer new leads to others in your network.

- Use the downtime to upgrade your onboarding process, automate more or work on the client experience.

All of this keeps your reputation strong, even if you're not taking on new work right now.

Use Capacity Tracking to Stay on Top of Your Workload

Track:

Metric	Description
Active Clients	Number of clients currently being served
Hours per client	Average monthly time commitment
Total billable hours	Your monthly service ceiling
Admin hours	Time spent on non-client tasks
Buffer margin	Extra time for emergencies or growth

If your workload constantly maxes you out, that's your signal to pause or make some changes.

Bottom line: Saying "no" isn't giving up. It's just being smart. You're protecting your energy, your reputation and your ability to grow without burning out.

Raising Rates with Existing Clients

Raising your rates isn't just about making more money. It's about showing how much you've grown, how much better you are at what you do and the extra value you bring to your clients. Still, some bookkeepers do feel nervous about raising prices for existing clients. They worry that people will get upset or leave. However, if you're upfront and professional about it, most clients will get it and stick around.

How do you raise your rates without it turning into a headache for everyone?

Why Raising Rates Matters

- You've become better at your job. Your systems run more smoothly. The quality of your work has leveled up.

- Costs keep climbing so it's natural that your pricing needs to keep up, too.

- You're giving clients more than you did when you started.

- You're getting close to full capacity; it makes sense to focus on the most profitable work.

- You want to grow your business without burning out.

If you haven't looked at your rates in the last year, now's the time.

When to Make the Move

Pick a moment that feels right and respectful, like:

- The start of a new financial year or quarter.

- After finishing a big project or clean-up.

- When you're renewing a contract or retainer.

- Once you've upgraded your systems or added new services.

- When you're bringing on new clients at higher rates.

And always—give them at least 30 days' notice. Nobody likes a surprise price hike halfway through the month.

How to Talk About It

Keep your message straightforward, positive and focused on your client.

Here's a way to say it:

"My services now include [short summary of added value] so I'm updating my pricing to match the level of support I provide. Starting [date], your new monthly rate will be [new rate]. I really appreciate your partnership and I'm committed to giving you the same high-quality service you expect."

Or maybe:

"To keep offering personal, timely support, I'm adjusting my rates for everyone. Your new rate kicks in on [date]. If you have any questions, I'm here."

Don't apologise—you haven't done anything wrong.

If a Client Pushes Back

If someone's unsure:

- Offer a smaller package with fewer services.

- Let the increase happen gradually over a couple of months.

- Thank them for their loyalty with a one-time discount.

- Remind them of the value they get.

Being flexible shows you care but don't sacrifice your own business health just to keep everyone happy.

Track the Impact of Your Rate Hike

Monitor:

Metric	Description
Clients retained	Who accepted the new rate
Clients lost	Who declined or paused service
Revenue change	Monthly income before and after
Time saved	Fewer clients at higher rates = more margin

You'll usually make more money working fewer hours—and start attracting clients who actually fit what you offer.

Here's the point: The real risk isn't raising your rates; it's staying stuck at the low end. When you speak up with clarity and confidence you respect your own growth, serve your clients better and build a business that really supports your life.

Figuring Out Your Perfect Client Load

Growing your bookkeeping business isn't just about chasing more clients. It's about knowing exactly how many you can handle without running yourself into the ground.

Your ideal client load sits right where your income goals, energy and quality of service line up. If you get greedy and take on too many, you'll burn out quickly. Take on too few and your business won't really go anywhere. What you want is that balance: enough clients to meet your goals but not so many that you lose control of your schedule or your sanity.

How do you figure out that number? You should look at a few things.

What to Think About

The right client load depends on:

- The kind of work you do—monthly bookkeeping, quarterly check-ins, messy clean-up jobs, advisory gigs

- How much time each client really needs every month

- All the little admin tasks—onboarding, emails, invoicing, chasing for info

- Your own energy and schedule—what else is on your plate?

- Your income goals—what do you need and what do you want?

- How smooth your systems are—are things running themselves or are you buried in busywork?

It's not just about how much you can handle on paper. It's about building something you can actually keep up—month after month.

How to Figure Out Your Client Load Number

Start with a simple formula:

$$\text{Ideal Client Load} = \frac{\text{Available Monthly Hours} - \text{Admin Hours}}{\text{Average Hours per Client}}$$

Example:

- Available monthly hours: 80
- Admin and marketing time: 20
- Average client time: 5 hours

According to this example, the client load for one month would be 12.

This gives you a working estimate; you can refine it as your systems improve.

How to Tell You've Hit Your Sweet Spot

You're turning in great work, project after project. You have space in your week—not just for client stuff but for marketing, learning new things and actually taking a breather. You're making enough to hit your financial goals. You're not stuck in constant panic mode, juggling emergencies. You feel genuinely proud of how you treat your clients.

Basically, if you're thriving instead of just scraping by, you're right where you should be.

Review Regularly

Things change. Maybe you raise your rates, streamline your workflow, bring in help, tweak your services or narrow your focus. Every few months—say, every quarter or so—take a step back and see if your current workload still feels right. Adjust if you need to.

The takeaway: Your ideal client load isn't some set-in-stone number. It will shift as your business grows and changes. When you really know what works for you and stick to it, you'll end up with a business that's not just profitable but actually energising—and built to last.

Moving From Hustle Mode to a Business That Lasts

When you start your bookkeeping business, hustle mode just happens. You're the marketer, the bookkeeper, the admin, the salesperson—everything. You say "yes" to anything that gets your foot in the door. That's how you get moving but hustle mode isn't a forever thing. The habits that helped you get started can start to drag you down if you don't switch gears.

Shifting to a sustainable business means you stop running on adrenaline and start building with intention. You make choices instead of just reacting. You're not chasing every lead—you're picking the right ones.

What Hustle Mode Feels Like

- You say "yes" to every job, even when it's not a good fit.

- You're working late, skipping breaks, always "on".

- You're scrambling—onboarding, delivering, following up—sometimes all at once.

- You charge too little or do too much, just to show you're worth it.

- You feel as if your business controls you, not the other way around.

At first, all this feels exciting; after a while, it wears you down.

What a Sustainable Business Looks Like

- You set clear limits—on your time, the work you take and how you communicate.

- Your pricing and packages show what you're really worth.

- You set up systems that handle the repetitive stuff for you.

- You work with the right number of clients—enough for your income and sanity.

- You're not afraid to say "no" to work that doesn't fit.

- You carve out time to rest, learn and plan for the future.

Sustainability takes effort. You have to build it on purpose.

How to Make That Shift

1. Audit Your Time and Energy.

Track your hours. Notice what drains you and what fires you up, then start shaping your days around that.

2. Refine Your Offers.

Bundle your services. Draw some lines around what you do (and don't do). Price your work so it actually pays off.

3. Automate and Delegate.

Get tools for stuff like invoicing or scheduling. Hand off any tasks that don't need your unique touch.

4. Set Capacity Limits

Figure out how many clients you can serve well. When you hit your max, use a waitlist or send referrals elsewhere.

5. Build in Recovery

Block out breaks. Leave space for buffer weeks or days off. Your business should fit your life—not take it over.

Mindset Shifts That Make It Work

- From "I have to do everything" to "I get to design how this works."

- From "I need every client" to "I choose the right clients."

- From "I'll rest when I'm done" to "Rest belongs in the plan."

- From "Busy means I'm successful" to "Sustainable means I can grow."

You don't have to burn out to grow. You need clarity.

The Bottom Line

Hustle gets you rolling but sustainability builds something that lasts. When you stop chasing every opportunity and start choosing the right ones, you create a business that's profitable, energising and actually worth keeping.

Conclusion (90-Day Action Plan)

Here's a 90-Day Action Plan to help you land your first 10 bookkeeping clients. It's divided into three phases, each designed to get you moving without burning you out or pulling you away from the clients you actually want.

90-Day Action Plan: Get Your First 10 Bookkeeping Clients

Phase 1: Foundation & Visibility (Days 1–30)

Let's start by setting up your business so people trust you and understand what you offer.

- Nail down your services and pricing.

- Put together branded onboarding stuff—think a welcome packet, intake form, engagement letter.

- Launch a simple website or landing page with clear calls to action.

- Update your LinkedIn profile. Join some relevant business groups.

- Reach out to your warm contacts—friends, old coworkers, local businesses.

- Post 2-3 helpful bookkeeping tips each week on social media to build trust.

- Ask for a couple of testimonials from early supporters or beta clients.

- Set up a referral incentive and tell your network about it.

By the end of the month, you want at least 2–3 discovery calls booked and 1–2 clients on board.

Phase 2: Outreach & Conversion (Days 31–60)

Now it's time to get out there and turn leads into paying clients.

- Track your outreach in a simple CRM or spreadsheet.

- Send personalised messages to 30–50 prospects—email, LinkedIn, referrals, whatever works.

- Go to 1–2 networking events, in-person or online.

- Follow up with leads from Phase 1 using a set process.

- Offer a limited-time onboarding bonus, such as a free clean-up or report review.

- Share a mini case study or a client success story.

- Tweak your discovery call script and your proposal template.

- Get your name out there with a guest blog post or podcast.

Aim for 4–6 new clients signed by the end of this phase.

Phase 3: Systems & Scaling (Days 61–90)

It's time to tighten things up and get ready for more growth.

- Audit your time and figure out your ideal client load.

- Automate what you can—scheduling, invoicing, reminders.

- Set clear boundaries around your scope, communication and availability.

- Bump up your rates for new clients if demand is high.

- Set up a waitlist or referral system for extra leads.

- Share a client milestone or testimonial to keep building credibility.

- Check your conversion rates and tweak your outreach as needed.

- Celebrate your wins and make a plan for what's next.

By the end, you should have your final 2–4 clients and systems ready to scale.

Total Goal: 10 clients signed and a clear, sustainable path for growing your bookkeeping business.

Celebrating the Milestone

Hitting your first 10 bookkeeping clients? That's huge. Getting here took guts, stubborn consistency and a mountain of work that nobody else really sees. It doesn't matter if it took you a month or half a year — landing those clients changes everything. You've proven you can do this. Now, take a breath. This is your moment. Celebrate it.

Here's why it actually matters to stop and enjoy this win:

- You see how far you've come and that boosts your confidence.

- Celebrating keeps you from burning out — it shows you that the grind is worth it.

- It gives you a good memory to come back to when things get tough.

- You remember your "why," and that keeps you moving.

Celebrating isn't just for fun. It's a smart move for your business.

Ways to Celebrate Your First 10 Clients

Choose what feels authentic and energising:

Celebration Idea	Description
Personal reward	Treat yourself to something meaningful – a meal, a gadget or a getaway
Client appreciation	Send a thank-you note or small gift to each client
Social media shoutout	Share your milestone with your network – invite others to join your journey
Reflection journal entry	Write down what worked, what surprised you and what you're proud of
Vision board update	Refresh your goals and visuals for the next phase
Mini launch or announcement	Use the momentum to promote your next offer or package

This isn't just about having a moment to celebrate. It's about pulling everything you've learned together and building on it.

Pause Before You Grow

Give yourself half an hour, maybe an hour. Ask yourself:

- What actually got me here?

- Which habits or systems made the biggest impact?

- If I had to do it again, what would I change?

- Which clients gave me energy instead of draining it?

- Who do I want my next ten clients to be?

This kind of reflection turns a win into a plan.

Own Your Progress

Say it out loud if you have to:

"I built this. I'm proud of it."

"I earned every client by being clear, caring and consistent."

"This is just the start. I'm ready for what's next."

Let your celebration mean something. Make it a statement.

Here's What Matters:

Milestones aren't just boxes to check off. When you celebrate on purpose, you respect your own effort, boost your momentum and build a business you're actually proud of, not just one that keeps you busy.

What's Next for Your Bookkeeping Business

Landing your first ten clients is huge but don't stop there. Real growth means letting go of the constant scramble and getting intentional. If you want to double your clients, offer more services or start building a team, it's time to scale up—with focus, confidence and a plan.

Here's how you can grow your business without burning out:

1. Sharpen Your Services

- Figure out which services actually make you money and light you up.

- Drop the ones that drain you or don't pay off.

- Think about adding packages or new advisory options.

- Keep your best clients in mind and adjust as they grow.

Growth happens when you're clear, not when you keep piling things on.

2. Raise Your Rates the Smart Way

- Check your pricing every six to twelve months.

- Set new rates for new clients.

- Let existing clients know about increases honestly and ahead of time.

- Charge for your value, not just your hours.

Higher rates mean you need fewer clients and make more on each one.

3. Get Your Systems in Order

- Automate stuff like onboarding, invoicing and reporting.

- Write down how you do repeating tasks—make some SOPs.

- Use templates for emails, proposals and check-ins.

- Keep track of your time so you don't overload yourself.

Good systems give you room to grow.

4. Build Real Partnerships

- Team up with accountants, consultants or virtual assistant agencies.

- Join local business groups or get active in online communities.

- Offer referral bonuses to people who send good clients your way.

- Show up at industry events and webinars—grow your network.

Partnerships help you reach more people without working more hours.

5. Boost Your Brand

- Update your website and social profiles.

- Share your clients' success stories and testimonials.

- Put out helpful content—blogs, videos, guides.

- Show people you know your stuff in your niche.

People trust who they see. Trust brings growth.

6. Protect Your Energy

- Set boundaries around your working hours, your services and how people can contact you.

- Decide how many clients you want and stick to it.

- Take breaks. Reflect and recharge.

- Celebrate your wins and recognize your progress.

Your business should support your life, not take it over.

Bottom line: Growth isn't just about getting more clients. It's about building better systems, setting stronger boundaries and making sure your business lines up with what matters to you. When you scale on purpose, you don't just survive—you build something that lasts and actually feels good to run.

The Right Software and Tools for Your Bookkeeping Business

To start a bookkeeping business you'll need more than just spreadsheets. You want tools that handle accounting, manage clients, automate boring stuff and keep you connected.

Here's a list of software I recommend to help you stay organized, look professional and grow your business without losing your mind:

Bookkeeping & Accounting Software:

Tool	Best For...	Notes
QuickBooks Online	Small businesses & freelancers	Industry standard; great for client collaboration
Xero	Cloud-based bookkeeping	Clean interface; strong reporting tools
Wave Accounting	Solo Bookkeepers & startups	Ideal for basic service packages
Zoho Books	Growing businesses	Affordable, with strong automation features
FreshBooks	Sedrvice-based professionals	Easy invoicing and time tracking

Client Relationship Management:

Keep track of leads, onboard new clients and stay organized with their info:

- Dubsado works well for service businesses that need custom workflows.
- HubSpot CRM has a free plan and handles outreach and follow-ups easily.
- HoneyBook puts proposals, contracts and payments all in one place.

Workflow & Automation:

Cut down on repetitive work and keep things running smoothly:

- ClickUp or Trello give you visual boards to manage client projects and deadlines.
- Zapier connects your favorite apps so tasks like sending invoices happen automatically.
- Calendly makes scheduling calls and check-ins easy for everyone.
- Google Workspace covers email, file sharing and collaboration in one spot.

Reporting & Analytics:

Show clients real results and stay on top of your numbers:

- Fathom gives you detailed financial reports and KPI dashboards.
- Syft Analytics helps bookkeepers create visual reports and forecasts.
- Excel or Google Sheets let you build custom templates for tracking outreach, conversions and capacity.

Security & File Sharing:

Keep client documents safe and make sharing simple:

- Dropbox Business or Google Drive offer secure cloud storage and access controls.
- LastPass stores your passwords safely across all your tools.
- Canopy gives accountants a secure client portal and document management.

The bottom line: The right tools don't just save time—they make you look more professional and give clients a better experience. Start with the basics, pick what fits your style and upgrade as your business expands.

About the Author

As a long-time blogger and former retail store owner, Barry knows what it takes to build a business from the ground up. With firsthand experience running a retail business and a passion for helping others succeed, he created this resource to guide new bookkeepers through the early stages of client acquisition and service setup.

When he's not helping small businesses simplify their finances, you'll find him kayaking or diving into his latest non-fiction read. His writing blends practical advice with a personal touch, making bookkeeping feel less like a chore and more like a smart business move.

This ebook is his contribution to newly certified bookkeepers looking to turn their skills into a thriving and rewarding practice.

www.ingramcontent.com/pod-product-compliance
Lightning Source LLC
LaVergne TN
LVHW022229200926
848481LV00006B/2187
9798232536893